D1643918

THE LAST OF THE DOZEN

The Last of The Dozen

RICHARD ROSS MACKAY

WITH A FOREWORD BY
COUNTESS MOUNTBATTEN OF BURMA, CBE, CD, JP, DL

The Pentland Press
Edinburgh – Cambridge – Durham – USA

First published in 1996 by
The Pentland Press Ltd
1 Hutton Close,
South Church
Bishop Auckland
Durham

ISBN 1-85821-382-7

Typeset by Carnegie Publishing, 18 Maynard St, Preston
Printed and bound by Antony Rowe Ltd, Chippenham

I would like to dedicate this book to the men and women of the forgotten 14th Army of Burma. That brave band of brothers comprised of many races – British, Indian, Nepalese, Chinese, American, West African and Burmese. They fought the longest campaign of World War II against a cruel and determined enemy, suffering the highest percentage of men missing in action and never found, in any campaign.

The words with which King Robert the Bruce inspired his greatly outnumbered army before the historic battle of Bannockburn, Scotland in 1314, could aptly apply to these men.

We fight not for glory nor wealth,
but for freedom alone,
which no good man
gives up lightly

In more recent times the inscription on the 14th Army memorial at Kohima in Burma, where the Japanese Imperial Army suffered its greatest defeat in their military history, says it all!

When you go home,
Tell them of us and say,
For your tomorrow
We gave our today.

Contents

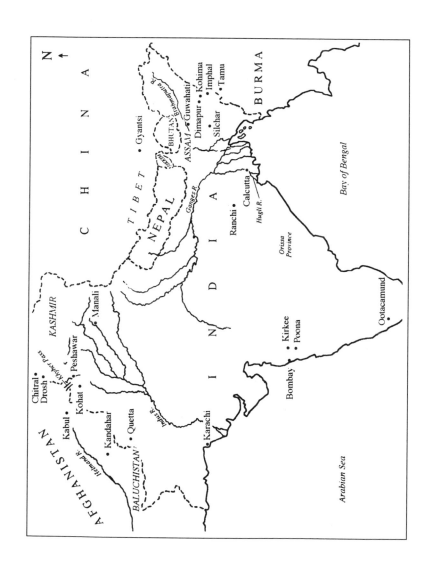

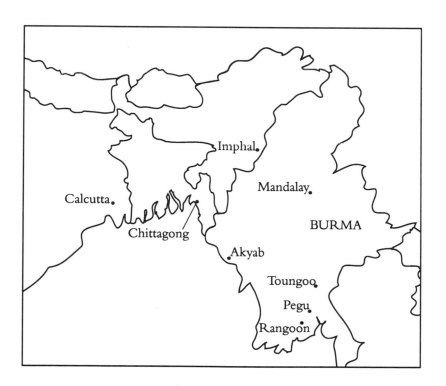

Imphal

Mandalay

Calcutta

Chittagong

BURMA

Akyab

Toungoo

Pegu

Rangoon

Foreword

I am pleased to have been asked to write a Foreword to this book because the author is a veteran of the Burma Campaign of the Second World War. Remarkably it is only in this fiftieth anniversary year of the end of the war that that so-called "Forgotten Army" and its veterans have at last been properly acknowledged for their amazing dogged courage and determination against all the odds, which achieved the final victory. My father, as the Supreme Allied Commander South East Asia, had the highest regard and affection for his 'Burma Stars'.

Richard MacKay showed these same qualities of endurance and determination after the war when fighting ill-health and set-backs so successfully that he achieved a very creditable, interesting, international career in the veterinary world.

He has shown us that the qualities that make a good soldier also make him a good civilian. The lessons learnt in hard wartime conditions can be put to good use in peacetime, and that a Burma Star can shine in different skies.

Mountbatten of Burma

Countess Mountbatten of Burma
CBE, CD, JP, DL.

Outline

Born a twin into a poor family of twelve children, the author briefly describes his childhood, school days and his first year in engineering at Glasgow University in 1942. He had to abandon his second year due to lack of funds. He then volunteered for the army in 1944 and trained in the Royal Engineers.

He describes his journey on a troop ship from Scotland to Bombay and his active service as a young soldier in Assam, Burma, Malaya and Singapore. He relates the amusing and also poignant experiences of a young soldier.

After release from the army in 1948 he worked on a dairy farm prior to going to Glasgow Veterinary School with the help of an ex-serviceman's grant. After only two months of study, and as a result of his ordeal in the Far East, he was hospitalized with pulmonary tuberculosis for two years. He describes the sadness and courage he experienced among his fellow patients.

After convalescence he returned to Glasgow Veterinary College in 1950, making his third start at a university education. He recalls his student days and the amusing pranks and incidents at college. He proceeded to postgraduate studies at Edinburgh then further training in laboratory techniques at Weybridge Veterinary Laboratory in England. He describes some of his amusing and poignant incidents in veterinary practice.

He worked for five years in the Veterinary Investigation Service in England and describes his diagnosis of four new animal diseases which he recorded and published. He then worked for one year at a large pharmaceutical company and was abruptly fired for refusing to conceal evidence of bacterial resistance to a new drug.

He emigrated to Canada in 1964 and worked for the Federal Government as a veterinary pathologist. During this time he also spent one year in Barbados for CIDA where he developed a functional laboratory for the island and other islands in the Caribbean community.

He represented his federal veterinary colleagues and negotiated the first collective bargaining agreement with the Federal Government of Canada. He then transferred to the Department of Health and Welfare where he became the Chief of the Human Safety Division of the Bureau of Veterinary Drugs.

He negotiated the first Free Trade agreement on veterinary drugs with the US government and also represented Canada at international meetings on veterinary drugs, including a select committee on veterinary drugs at a FAO/WHO (Food and Agriculture Organisation/World Health Organisation), meeting in Geneva.

On retirement from the Canadian Service he moved to Adelaide where he assisted the South Australian government and also acted as a consultant to the Commonwealth Government in Canberra. He now resides in Victoria BC where he acts as Welfare Officer for the local Burma Star Association assisting old comrades from the Burma campaign.

In his lifetime he worked for five different governments on three continents and he makes some observations and comparisons on the functions of the different civil service organisations and the factors which govern promotion and advancement.

CHAPTER I

Childhood and Youth

When you ask someone which first event in their life they can remember, you will find a great diversity of age for such recollection. They will vary from less than one year to over two years. Why we remember such early incidents is hard to say. Perhaps they are associated with joy, pain, fear or pride. My first recollections of my childhood was at about one year old. I was aware that there were two of us and dressed alike and generally always together. We had received new blue romper suits and we were lifted on to the table, side by side, and fussed over by my sisters – there were six of them. In fact our small rented home was incredibly busy and overcrowded, but at that time in 1925, I knew nothing else and this was normal.

This old two-storey sandstone building had about twenty apartments on each floor. They had two large bedrooms, a very large living-room and a small kitchen. The toilet was out in the stairwell and was shared by another family. There was no bathroom as such. Our bath consisted of a large round galvanized tub about four feet wide. Water was heated on an open coal fire or in a gas-fired boiler. We had no electricity, only coal-gas for cooking and lighting. Except for two sisters still at school, my four older brothers and six older sisters all worked. My father was an iron moulder and coremaker in a foundry, where he worked for over fifty years.

When I was about 5 years old, we moved to a new council

house with three bedrooms, kitchen, bathroom and large living-room. We had coal-gas and electricity. We also had a large garden which was of great value to my father who was a very good gardener. My grandfather had been head gardener to a large castle in Scotland. I remember being put into the bath with my twin brother for the first time. Normally I did not relish being scrubbed, but I enjoyed this new experience. The main disadvantage was my school was now one mile away, which meant I had to walk four miles per day to school. Sometimes after school I would also have to run errands for my mother, which meant another two miles. Six miles per day is a lot for a 5-year-old. Today it would be unthinkable. We were a poor hard-working family, and I never had very much. No bicycle or expensive toys. I had school clothes and Sunday clothes – kept only for the Sabbath day or special occasions. When my growth rate began to outstrip my Sunday clothes, they were quickly relegated to school use. Despite the overcrowding we were a happy family. There was always a lot of give and take between brothers and sisters, and teasing of the girls. There was never any obscene language. My old mother toiled endlessly to keep the home clean and running.

If my father was head of the family, my mother was its heart. Our meals were simple and generally made from inexpensive food. Somehow her soups and stews were more tasty and appetizing than present day food. Perhaps it was the home-grown vegetables and meat from grass-fed animals and fresh free-range eggs. Nothing was wasted. Perhaps it was also because I was too busy getting something to eat, that everything tasted so good. All I know is that this simple fare seemed much tastier than modern meals prepared by modern equipment and methods. I had chores to complete on a regular basis – cleaning my father's boots, running errands, etc. Generally, I came off worse than my twin, who was smaller than me, and often escaped doing his share. I never thought that was fair.

My school was a fairly old building, and all my junior school teachers were women. There was a reason for this. The First World War had killed many young men, and there were numerous unmarried women in Scotland. Many of these maiden ladies went into teaching. They were "old maids" as we called them in Scotland. However, they became very dedicated teachers. You cannot beat the dedication of the "Old Maid". I owe a great debt to these ladies. They taught me well.

When I was 8 or 9 years old I started to frequent a local dairy farm and soon became very interested in livestock and farming. They never paid me, but fed me very well. Farmers are notoriously mean with money but generous otherwise. At 11 I was allowed to drive an old Fordson tractor which had no brakes – only a clutch and three forward gears. As time passed I was learning a great deal about animals and farming. I had a favourite old horse, Tommy, who was a gentle giant. He had a bad hind foot which bothered him a lot. I remember taking him to the blacksmith to have him shod.

The blacksmith was a kindly old man, and I told him about the sore foot, and asked if he could help him. I remember he looked at me earnestly and said, "You really like that old horse? Well! We will see what we can do for him." He removed the old shoe and cleaned up the frog. He then made a nice leather pad to fit over the foot and added some pine tar to keep it clean. Old Tommy walked just fine on his new shoe, and I thanked the old blacksmith sincerely. I believe that was the incident that kindled my interest in veterinary work. I remember when old Tommy collapsed one summer day in a field, and could not get up. He was to be shot right where he lay, then taken away for dog meat. I bathed his fly-ridden eyes and squeezed some fresh cold water into his mouth from a rag. He grunted in appreciation. I did not watch him being shot and hauled away. It was a very sad end for a faithful old servant.

Farm work was hard labour, and I learned a great deal. I learned how to tend animals and poultry how to feed and when to feed them, their natural cycles and habits. In fact, a great deal of useful knowledge I would not acquire at the veterinary school. Most of all I learned how to converse with stock owners. This was something that farmers often sensed when you first met them.

At age 12 I moved into high school which was part of the same school building. I studied French, Latin, English, mathematics, history, geography and science. My eldest brother continually exhorted me to stay at school and not to leave at 14, which was the minimum age for leaving. He made a very strong case for higher education, although my poor parents did not encourage me either way. My twin brother left as soon as he was 14 and found work as an apprentice engineer in a local foundry. He had lots of leisure time while I had large amounts of homework. However, it was already evident to me that higher education would be necessary, if I was to obtain a well-paid job or become a professional. My twin had lots of money to spend, and after work or on weekends he was free to enjoy life and do whatever he liked.

My nose was to the grindstone, and I had little money to spend. My sisters got married in quick succession and the available living space in our overcrowded home was of great benefit. Then the dreaded day arrived and suddenly we were at war with Nazi Germany. I can recall my father's wish, that it would be all over before my twin and I became military age. It was wishful thinking indeed, as time would tell. My two oldest brothers both volunteered for the RAF and left home. My third brother and one sister also joined the RAF and the ATS (women's army). The husbands of four of my sisters were also called for service in the army or RAF. We were reduced from a large family of six sons and six daughters, down to my twin and myself. We had both joined the ATC (Air Training Corps.) which trained boys for the RAF. I could receive and send messages by Morse code. I could even plot a course by compass for an aircraft. I became adept at aircraft recognition. Later, when I was 16, I joined the Home Guard and had a rifle and bayonet kept at home, in case of invasion by Germany. I was part of a "Smith" gun crew. This weapon was a small artillery piece which fired a 6 pound shell and could be used as an anti-tank weapon. My job was to set the range and elevation of the gun. Most of our Home Guard unit were old soldiers above military age, while I was young and very fit. On manoeuvres I was always ahead of everyone. I realized that fitness was very important for a soldier in action.

I completed my high school final exams before I was 16 years of age and was keen to go to university but the cost was going to be very high for me and my poor family. I decided that engineering was my best bet financially, since one did four six-month terms of study and four six-month spells of practical work for which one received apprentice wages. I worked all summer on a farm to save money and applied for as many scholarships as I could find. Finally, I received £30 from Stirlingshire County Education Department, £18 from the

Carnegie Trust and £10 from the Clan MacKay Society. If I packed a lunch and travelled to Glasgow by bus on a weekly ticket I would just make it financially with the help of my summer savings plus bursaries.

Having completed my first year of engineering at Glasgow University before I became 17 years of age, with almost no money to spare, I worked all summer in a Glasgow shipyard drawing office until my second year was about to begin. Alas, I was not able to afford the expense and would need to wait another year. During this time our country was under great strain due to the course of the war and I decided to volunteer for the army and serve my country. Perhaps I could have been exempted from National Service, but my volunteering seemed the correct thing to do, as my native land Scotland was in danger of a German invasion. With all the relatively flat areas dotted with wooden poles to deter enemy gliders from landing.

These were momentous times. I watched the severe bombing of Clydebank on two consecutive clear nights as German bombers droned overhead all night. We did what we could for the poor bombed-out refugees, who were sent to our small town for shelter. We were very short of mattresses for temporary billets in huts, schools, golf-club houses, etc. I asked my farmer friend to help, and we supplied some very nice soft oat straw to fill temporary mattresses. At least these poor families could have a soft place to rest. I was very impressed by the courage and spirit of these Glaswegians, I just could not imagine how Hitler would ever subdue such people. It was doomed to failure.

I was soon called up for the army and reported to Maryhill Barracks in Glasgow – only twenty miles from home. I was to spend six weeks there doing basic training – mostly squad drill, which had great emphasis in the army. We were packed like sardines into small wooden huts with two-tier wooden beds every two or three feet. We were too tightly housed and soon were installed in larger huts. I well remember a cockney Sergeant coming into our new hut and inquiring from a refined English lad, "How do you like your new 'ut?" He replied it was more capacious. The sergeant immediately replied, "More room too, ain't there." My army service had finally begun.

We were all given tests for the course of a whole day. They were on general knowledge, simple mathematics, some trigonometry, writing skills, and practical skills, e. g., reconstructing a bicycle pump, etc. Nothing was too advanced or difficult. These were placement or aptitude tests. One older man from Central Europe was posted to the Intelligence Corps. to everyone's surprise. He was fluent in several European languages. I was destined for the Royal Engineers, which was no surprise to me and I was satisfied with this posting. We had quite a competitive spirit between the different platoons in training. I believe the platoon sergeants were the main cause of this, as they were graded on comparative results of their platoons. We had a sports day and there was a marathon run for several miles along the banks of the Forth and Clyde canal which passed through this area of Glasgow. I tried very hard to win this race, but I was against a marathon runner, whom I just could not overtake at the finish line. I received ten shillings as second prize (a week's army pay) from the CO and a 48-hour pass which allowed me to go home and visit my parents about twenty-five miles away. My old platoon sergeant of the Seaforth Highlanders was very pleased and thumped me heartily on the back as I crossed the finish in second place.

Army training was not all fun and games. We were taught

to shoot – first with 22 rifles indoors, then at field targets with our 303 army rifles. Here I had an unpleasant experience. The army, in its wisdom, supplies only rifles for use with your right hand for reloading and firing off your right shoulder. My right eye was useless, more like a light sensitive cell than an eye. However, I had a very good left eye and had been taught by an old soldier in the Home Guard how to fire off my left shoulder and reload with the heel of my left hand. This meant that my legs were spread in the opposite direction to give balance. When I was in position to fire at the target 200 yards away, an irate sergeant came along and yelled at me and kicked my legs to move me into the accepted position. I tried to explain but was rudely told to shut up. Fortunately a major came along and said, "No, let the man speak, Sergeant."

I explained my difficulty, but assured the Major I could perform quite well from my left eye, as I had been taught to do so by an old First World War veteran. He was intrigued and the whole company rested while I had to fire five rounds on my own at the target. I was very nervous but determined. My first shot was an "outer" – that is on the outer ring of the target. I steadied myself and my next shot was an "inner", then three bull's-eyes in a row. The officer immediately told this Sergeant that if he can shoot like that off his left shoulder, let them all shoot that way. Of course this bird brain told me later he would get me for this. My old Seaforth Highlander Sergeant soon assured me he would not bother me. Sometimes you wonder just how these men are selected to lead. In any case, I was soon on my way to engineer training in Lancashire on the river Ribble.

We were billeted in an old weaving mill in a huge multi-storey building with stone floors and a narrow steep stone stairway. Only one soldier could ascend or descend at a time, and there were hundreds of us in the building. We had to descend to a large mess hall for our meals – if you could call them that! We had several ATS girls working as cooks. We were continually exhorted by an officer to vacate the mess hall as soon as possible, as there were numerous men waiting their turn at the trough. I recall one dinner time we were having boiled cabbage, spuds and sausage. Great consternation erupted – one soldier had found a condom in his cabbage and was holding it up on his fork for all to see. I believe the pigs had a feast on the swill that day. For days to come we examined our dinner carefully much to this officer's annoyance.

Some of the training became boring. A Bailey bridge was a wonderful invention and proved a major factor in every army campaign. It was like a Meccano set, easy to assemble and launch over a gap. You merely ensured enough counterweight to land it on the other side on a launching ramp. Over water it was more complex and required floating pontoons at regular intervals until you reached the far bank. After a while the physical labour involved in assembling the bridge became very boring.

The most interesting and challenging part of training was in mines, demolitions and booby-traps. It was fine dealing with safe mines, but it was a deadly game when it came to the real thing. I think I gave this training my full attention, which was to serve me well on active service. There was really no limit to the ingenuity which could be applied to booby-traps. One day we were given an old house to booby-trap as we wished. Small BT signs were placed in the ground around it, which was standard practice. We had to booby-trap inside these signs and were challenged by a bumptious corporal, that he could find and neutralize the lot. My mate and I took up his challenge. We decided to run a small wire from the bottom tip of the BT sign, under the ground to a small pull igniter with a small charge attached to it. The instructor, of course, found them all except our effort and insisted it must be outside the area. We assured him it was not outside. Eventually he disdainfully began picking up the BT signs and of course set off our little charge. These was a great cheer from the men and a very deflated corporal. Later this lesson would not be lost on me in Burma.

One day as we were nearing the end of our thirteen weeks of engineer training I was ordered to report to my CO at my company office. He was a fat overweight major and very condescending. He informed me I had been selected for WOSB. When I inquired what that meant he disdainfully told me, as if I should have known, War Office Selection Board (for commissions). Later I was among several other sappers addressed by this major on being an officer. He told us it was our duty to become officers, if we had money, or position in society. I just could not believe my ears. Later I would discover he was not joking. It seemed they were deemed to be important qualifications to be leaders of men. I was soon given preferential dental treatment and another medical examination. I was then dispatched to a large country house near Warrington in Lancashire along with about half a dozen other men. These were mainly public school types, which in England really means private school boys. I guess I was there since I had at least one year of engineering at Glasgow University besides a good Scottish Higher School Leaving Certificate, which was probably worth more than an English Matriculation Certificate. We were there for a few days and lived in nice rooms with sheets and tablecloths, etc. We ate next to the officer staff. It was all very genteel and civilized. The tests we were given were not too difficult and sometimes even childish puzzles. We had numerous interviews and even psychiatric sessions. I well remember one overweight fat major with his flabby jowls hanging over his collar. He was very interested in my social background. What school did I go to?

"Denny Public School, sir."

"Oh! You went to a public school?"

"Yes, sir, but in Scotland that is a council school and not a private school."

"But surely you did not go to university from a council school?"

"Of course, sir – why not? My Scottish Leaving Certificate is the standard for entry to any Scottish university. English students must pass the University Preliminary Examination and often fail it."

"Really! What does your father do?"

"He is a moulder and coremaker, sir."

"What is that?"

I had to explain that it was an iron foundry tradesman.

"But does he own the place?"

"No, sir, he is a tradesman."

I was beginning to get irate.

Later it was decided somehow that I was unsuitable for a commission in the engineers, but I could go to an Infantry Regiment; and I could even choose a Scottish regiment like the Argyles which was my local regiment. I was very annoyed. It was clear to me that these regiments like the Argyles who invariably bore the brunt of an attack, were short of officer cannon fodder. I said I had four brothers and two sisters and four brothers-in-law in the forces, and did not wish to add to my parents' anxiety, to be immediately told, it was my duty. I asked, how would I tell that to my old mother, and was told in a haughty manner it was my duty to fight for England. I countered that I was not fighting for England but for Scotland and was promptly informed it was the same thing.

This was the final insult. I pointed out I was of Highland stock and we were brought up to honour our clan and Scotland. Death before dishonour was our motto. It must have been disturbing for this intellectual wilderness to be outdone by an 18-year-old from a working class background. It was no secret that I would be rejected for a commission, while other well-heeled tits were found acceptable and it prompted serious reservations as to what we were fighting to preserve in the UK. Later I was to encounter some useless officers who were literally carried by their men. In fairness, there were a few excellent officers well worthy of their rank.

When I returned to my unit my Colonel sent for me to give me the bad news – which I already knew. He merely said I was not suitable, but had good potential to be an NCO – non commissioned officer. This was suppose to placate me. I said nothing, in case I would be charged with insubordination; but I knew then that my social background was far more important than my ability. However, in the Far East my ability kept me alive.

After the war we often agreed, we won despite our officers. I doubt very much if Britain learned a lesson, but as science progresses and warfare becomes more and more technical, there will be no place for imbecilic sons of aristocracy in field units of the army. The Navy and RAF have already reached that stage.

At least my training was over and I prepared for posting to a unit of Field Engineers and active service.

CHAPTER 2

Active Service

The long hard days of military training were over, six weeks of basic training plus thirteen weeks of sapper training in the Royal Engineers.

By now I had learned how to use a rifle and bayonet, fire a Bren gun and a Sten sub-machine-gun, arm and throw a live hand grenade, recognise German, Italian and British tanks and aircraft, detect and disarm booby-traps and land-mines, (German, Italian, Hungarian and British) and of course army drill. The latter seemed to have occupied more time than the more technical items which were destined to be of vital importance to my survival. Ironically, no one had ever shown me a Japanese land-mine, tank or aircraft. I recall asking the sergeant instructor in training about Japanese mines, and he sheepishly informed me he did not have one. When asked what one looked like, he hesitantly said it was quite similar to our own mine which was like a round biscuit tin, about one foot in diameter. As for recognizing Japanese aircraft, no one had a clue – although as a boy of 15 or 16 years I knew the Zero fighter plane and the three-engine Mitsubishi bomber from boys' magazines. In short, we had no knowledge of anything Japanese although I had long suspected I would be destined for the Far East theatre of war. This incredible lack of knowledge of our potential enemy was symbolic of the whole attitude to the war in the Far East. Later I was to realize that the 14th Army was justly nicknamed the Forgotten 14th.

Indeed, Lord Mountbatten, when he came to review his troops hailed them with the words, "Of course you are the Forgotten 14th Army – no one has ever even heard of you." This brand of top-brass "bull" was somehow supposed to placate us. We were not amused.

Besides the training in booby-traps and mines we were trained to blow holes or *camouflet* roads or tracks and also to demolish buildings, bunkers, and railway lines. At one time we had succeeded in blowing rocks on to the roof of a shepherd's cottage on the Yorkshire moors. This was the result of a miscalculation of the charge used, according to the Court of Inquiry. In reality, it was due to an overzealous lance-corporal instructor who wished to out-bang the other instructors. However, the lesson was not lost on me and was to be of use later in my active service.

The most important part of my training was in bridge building. I knew how to build a Bailey bridge over land or over water. I learned how to calculate the gap to be bridged without crossing the gap. I knew the various classifications, i.e. tonnage permitted for the various types of Bailey bridge from single truss, single storey to triple-triple. I also knew that the easiest job was the down-stream pin-man who inserted the pins to connect the Bailey panels together. Generally though, this task was allocated to a small lightweight sapper. We had also trained on folding-boat equipment bridges which were by then obsolete and only used as a temporary bridge unlike the Bailey bridge which was probably the best invention of the entire war and proved to be a major factor in the defeat of the Imperial Japanese Army in Burma.

As soon as my training was completed I was posted with three of the 120 men I had trained with to join an engineer company at Aldershot near London. This engineer unit was mobilizing there in preparation for going overseas. I had no idea how the army selected us, if indeed they used any form of selection at all. The town was an old military base close to the southern edge of London, with numerous dismal looking barracks surrounded by enormous barrack squares. Obviously the army emphasis was on squad drill with all its discipline dating back to Crimea and beyond. The Army Council was still living in the past and ignoring the tremendous technical advances which had been made in military manoeuvres and techniques. Perhaps they believed that the ability to march and countermarch on these squares would somehow prepare us to move through the thick, uncharted jungles of southeast Asia and defeat the enemy!

Aldershot was indeed a dreary town. No doubt the years of occupation by the military had hardened the inhabitants towards rough, uncouth soldiers. This was unlike many other towns in Britain where servicemen were treated well, and indeed feted in places like Glasgow, as if they were their own sons. In Glasgow, when in uniform, you could travel anywhere by bus, tram or underground for one penny. However, it was almost impossible to get the attention of the conductress or "clippie" as she was known, to take your fare. No one ever requested to see your ticket. In Aldershot I was once travelling on a bus and unfortunately I had only a five-pound note, a Scottish one at that which was twice the size of the Bank of England counterpart. This caused consternation in the bus which quickly came to a halt while the conductor, driver and finally an inspector examined this bank note from every angle as if they were currency experts. Finally, they asked me to leave the bus and I refused. Subsequently, an elderly gentleman in a hurry paid my fare to avoid any delay.

I had made my point that Scottish currency had at least equal value to English and was legal tender. Regrettably, the town of Aldershot had been badly damaged previously by Canadian Troops stationed there for a time. These men were obviously fully trained and bored while they awaited posting. The cool and frosty reserve of the town inhabitants was no doubt due to the long standing presence of common soldiery in the town and their somewhat ribald behaviour. The reactions of the Canadians, although inexcusable was nevertheless understandable from men who had all volunteered to fight for Britain. Needless to say the aftermath of this regrettable incident was felt for some time afterwards and Aldershot was not a friendly place to be.

We were at once billeted in brick buildings, ten to a unit with army beds, blankets and a pot-bellied stove in the middle of the room. We had one army table and a wooden wardrobe beside each bed. This was relative luxury after training but there was no fuel for the stove and it was 0°C outside. With true engineering ingenuity we quickly dismantled an old wardrobe with our bayonets and sapper jack-knives and soon we had a nice warm fire with no trace of the missing wardrobe. After all we were taught to improvise and be self-reliant.

Soon we were all issued with tropical kit which consisted of khaki drill pants, shorts and bush shorts. This was a pantomime as all the slacks had narrow legs and had obviously been issued to troops in Victoria times. We were truly soldiers of the Queen – Victoria that is, and it was not even Hallowe'en!

As in all army units there was considerable speculation and rumour as to our eventual destination. No one really knew, which made the rumours worse. My old pal from training days was a Londoner and had been a surveyor in civvy street. We discussed the possibilities. We agreed khaki drill was not for Europe and the Second Front, but it could be for North Africa or the Middle East theatre. However, that seemed unlikely as there were ample troops there already and the conflict was over. That left Australia and New Zealand where the Japanese were threatening. Burma was a possibility, but our gear would have been olive-green for there. That left India as the main possibility. We would need to wait and see because in those army days we were treated like mushrooms, i.e. kept in the dark and fed on horse manure!

After three days in Aldershot, we were all given leave and travel warrants with strict orders to be back within four days. For me this was a cruel joke as a scheduled train from London to Glasgow could take sixteen hours or more to make the journey so I would have, with luck, forty-eight hours at home before returning. This was undoubtedly embarkation leave and God knows when I would return home again – if ever. I made my protest to a toffee-nosed English captain who shrugged it off as bad luck being born so far north. I pointed out that this was bad only related to this journey and he immediately told me I was being insubordinate. I did not apologise and he dismissed me disdainfully. The journey to Scotland seemed interminable and most of the way I had no seat and slept in the corridor of the carriage. The first-class carriages of course were fully occupied by officers and civilians.

When I eventually arrived home my old mother was very happy to see me, and see me looking very fit and well. I did not tell her I had to return after two nights at home as I fervently prayed for an extension of embarkation leave. Happily, I received a telegram the second day home, granting me another full week of leave. This was a great gift for my mother as she had five sons, two daughters and four sons-in-law all in the armed forces. From a busy home with six sons and six daughters she was reduced to only one married son who lived with his wife in a small town. It was a great transformation for her and quite an ordeal. She once told me she liked getting mail but also dreaded the postman in case it meant disaster. I guess if she had been in Russia, she would have been a Hero of the Soviet Union for her own private army. Of course, I did not tell her I was on embarkation leave. Indeed I told her nothing at all; but my old dad knew only too well I was on my way to war. On the last day he did a peculiar thing – he came up to Glasgow with me on the bus and we parted at the bus station and not at the railway station where I was headed. We shook hands and I left down the street for the railway station. He knew the score, yet never mentioned it. I recalled the days as a poor student when I had walked these same streets on my way to my university classes in order to save a few pennies on tram fare. Now that was the stiff upper lip, but not the English version.

Back in Aldershot, in only a matter of days we were given several inoculations for diseases, held final kit inspections, and made wills etc. Meanwhile we heard nightly, the drone of RAF bombers going to and coming from Germany on their bombing missions.

At last the big day arrived and we were trucked to the railway station and packed like sheep into a troop train. We took it in turn to sit down. By now the camaraderie of fighting men was beginning to show. We had been given very strict instructions that no mail was to be sent by us from now onwards until further notice. The train crawled its way up the east coast to Edinburgh, which baffled all the pundits as to our destination. It was then headed westward to Glasgow where we had a quick snack on a railway platform and then on to Greenock on the Clyde estuary. As we trundled slowly and haltingly towards Greenock some of the men passed letters to passers-by near the railway track for posting to their relatives. Ah, well, for the army authorities, the best laid schemes o'mice and men gang aft a-gley, but I was sure no harm was done. After all the presence of a large convoy of ships forming up for days in the Firth of Clyde could hardly be concealed and was a common occurrence.

We were herded from the troop train in what can only be described as organized chaos. Then on to the tenders which plied their way to and from a large, 30,000-ton liner lying at anchor amongst other vessels. Soon we were herded up a gang plank into the bowels of the great liner accompanied by bleating noises from the more carefree members of our unit. We were soon to realize that these noises were not altogether inappropriate as we descended to near the tank top or double bottom of this great liner – F Deck. The troop deck was very clean, almost sterile and had about eight foot headroom with no portholes. We were below the water-line, obviously, and if torpedoed we were done for. There were numerous racks on the ceiling to stow kit and large 4-foot wide tables about four feet apart on each side of the deck. These had adjoining benches at which we would sit, i.e. mess tables, although they were used to sleep on as well. All around there were mattresses and also hammocks slung from ceiling hooks for the same purpose. Behind a bulkhead were ablutions – in army parlance – toilets, showers and washing facilities.

We quickly acquired a place at a table, twelve men to a table, and claimed a mattress or hammock. Once settled my old buddy from London and I had a little confab and decided before anything became settled or regulated we would explore the ship before the guards were posted. This was a good move as we were able to ascertain how the officers would live. All on upper decks in nice air-conditioned cabins with one to four men to each cabin depending on the size of the unit. Nice dining area with waiter service of course. We tried to find some crew members to ask where we were headed, but they obviously knew nothing except they expected a long voyage, four, five or even six weeks at sea. This was intriguing as Australia now seemed a definite possibility. We soon settled down to the routine. Meals were prepared on the upper deck galley and carried below by two men per table in large dixies. The NCO at each table dished out the grub and passed it along the table accompanied by the usual comments from the known comedians.

It was going to be a long dreary journey and with this in mind I had a good idea. My mate and I volunteered for duty on top. Of course the army with its perchant for putting square pegs in round holes, decided to assign us as engineers to the 4-inch gun on the stern of the weather deck of the ship. We seized the chance as volunteers and were assigned, despite the presence of Royal Artillery units on board. The big 4-inch gun was not a complicated gun. We soon mastered its traverse and elevation which was done by hand. We also acquired knowledge of the range-finder although this was done separately and relayed to us by the crew. The loading was fairly simple and the whole drill was given to us by the ship's crew who had been trained for this job by the navy. This gun duty gave us a great deal of space and privacy and no other duties such as guard duty, fire picket, ablution cleaning etc. A smart move, when I think of it, to be up in the fresh air and not down in the cesspit with hundreds of other men.

For five long days we waited in the Clyde watching the lights of Greenock and the beautiful Clyde estuary with the mountains in the background. One poor lad belonged to Greenock and said he could actually see his home.

There is an old custom – never to set sail on a Friday, and sure enough we awoke one Saturday morning to find ourselves at sea and rolling about in gale force winds. It was chaotic on the mess deck. Many men were very seasick and stood hungover in the washroom leaning against the wall which served as a urinal. As the volume of vomit increased it was a disgusting sight as it flowed back and forth in the trough with the roll of the great liner. Men were becoming very seasick and disorientated. Some of the worst cases had little wish to live as they were so dejected and ill. Of course, the army in its wisdom supplied greasy bacon and fried eggs for breakfast, the very sight of which sent men scurrying and swaying for the ablutions to contribute to the already overloaded runnoff channel. Fortunately, my mate and I were unaffected by the ship's roll and we ate heartily on the ample unused rations.

For the next three days the seas were very rough as we sailed into strong westerly winds. It was a strict rule that everyone must have his life-jacket with him at all times. Space on the weather deck was limited and we were warned repeatedly to stay clear of the ships rails. If we were swept overboard the ship would *not* stop to pick us up and our chances of rescue by the ships in the convoy were very slim indeed. As far as I could see in the weather there were three lines of ships in the convoy and we were in the middle of the middle lane, i.e. we were obviously the biggest target for submarines.

At one daily roll-call a man was missing and could not be found. He was a slight, delicate lad of 19 and had been very seasick and depressed. Since I had talked to him a little I was questioned by our captain about him. I described him as a bit of a loner and quiet in nature. My officer repeatedly asked me where I last saw him. I told him I did not think he had gone overboard intentionally or otherwise and suggested he should consider that the lad had probably holed up somewhere on the ship as he was very seasick. I was then given five more men to conduct a search for the missing sapper. I explained that if I was him I would try to find a secure place to rest until I had recovered.

We searched everywhere on all decks even in the out of bounds areas, much to the annoyance of some officers.

Finally, I went back to the place I last saw him, which was on the weather deck at the stern of the ship, and checked the lifeboats and rafts without success. Then I spotted a large coil of rope used to dock the ship. This was coiled in a neat roll about four feet high like a huge doughnut. Sure enough, down in the bottom of the coil lay the poor young lad coiled up in the foetal position. He looked gaunt and frozen. His battledress was soiled with vomit and he was in terrible shape. We soon had him down in the sick-bay where the medics gave him immediate attention. In a few days he would be OK. My captain was more anxious to know how I found him. I explained, if I had been in his shoes, that is where I would have gone. This explanation was not well received, it was too logical and not covered in army regulations.

The weather soon improved and my mate and I set about estimating our position at sea. The army, of course, gave us no information at all as to our destination. The authorities

however did something quite illogical considering all the se-
crecy – they announced the ship's daily run in nautical miles.
With the aid of a small pocket book which contained a few
small scale maps we set about calculating our position and
course. For the first four days we were definitely heading
southwest according to the position of the sun. Perhaps after
all we were headed towards the Panama Canal and on to
Australia or New Zealand. However, the next morning we
went up on deck and soon discovered we were now steaming
due east in almost an about turn. There was now no doubt
that we were heading for Gibraltar and the Mediterranean.

Before long we spotted small fishing vessels, probably Por-
tuguese, and also a few sea birds. By now the convoy lines
appeared closer in and we could almost see our escorting
frigates. The arrival of a Sunderland flying boat on submarine
patrol convinced us that Gibraltar was not far off. Next day,
the little navy frigates steamed up alongside our troop ship but
going in the opposite direction – back home. They hooted
loudly as they passed, as a final farewell – we gave them a
cheer and a wave. Soon a new escort of ships and planes took
over as we steamed past the mighty Rock of Gibraltar with
the whole Mediterranean fleet anchored near its base. We were
now in the Mediterranean.

My guess of India as our destination was beginning to look
right on. The Mediterranean was fairly calm and appeared to
be really blue and pleasant. The sun was warm and invigorating.
Up on the gun platform we really had a cushy number, as the
troops called it.

We did have one bit of excitement during a boat drill when
everyone was supposed to muster at their appointed boat
stations in case of emergency. A submarine was spotted up

ahead of us and, of course, we were at full alert. It was a strange sight, it was on the surface and appeared to be painted with long bands of dull yellow against the grey hull. Yet at a distance you could scarcely see it. It was a US sub and quickly flashed a message to the convoy. From my meagre knowledge of Morse code gained in the Air Training Corps as a boy, I interpreted the message – "Have you any Wrens on board?" Only Americans would have sent such a message. I was unable to see the reply.

The excitement was soon over and we steamed on past Malta and then quite close to Linosa and Pantellaria – two small islands between the toe of Italy and the North Africa coast. At least we had a good fix and we estimated we would make Port Said in two days; we were right on.

We dropped anchor in Port Said near the Suez Canal entrance. Port holes were opened wide. A fleet of small Arab craft greeted our arrival, affectionately known to the troops as bum boats. I never did get the name connection, but British troops invariably label things and places with outlandish names.

We had hoped for shore leave but our chances were remote. The Arab vendors plied their wares night and day, mostly dates, leather handbags and Turkish delight, not forgetting Spanish Fly which was an aphrodisiac. Needless to say it was hardly necessary or likely to be of use in a boat load of soldiers. Still the odd zealot purchased some out of curiosity.

We took on board four Arabs with two canoes. This intrigued me but I soon realized their purpose. The Suez Canal was relatively narrow in places and of course very busy. When we had to pass another ship these Arabs went ashore with their canoes and towed a large rope to the bank where it was secured to bollards. The great ship then winched herself sideways to

allow the smaller ship to pass, a neat manoeuvre. In the middle
of the canal we passed through the Bitter Lakes which were
so called because of their high salt content. Here the shipping
lanes were marked with red and green lights and it was just
like a roadway with traffic lights, especially at night. By day
we could see the traffic on the roadway running along the
canal bank. The British had a large military base near Port
Suez at the southern end of the Canal. The locals ran their
camels much faster than the ship to the cheers of the troops.
The common Arab response was always the same. The Arab
would lift his long robes up around his arm pits and present
his genitals rather like an army inspection for venereal disease.
This evoked raucous laughter and ribald remarks from the
troops. It was a culture shock!

At the southern end of the Canal we dropped anchor at
Port Suez where the ship took on water and provisions. Fresh
fruit and vegetables were being loaded from the small Arab
crafts. We soon cashed in on this operation. I obtained a small
carton box from the ship's canteen and obtained a piece of
1-inch rope from a lifeboat. We selected a port hole near the
Arab boats and lowered our box with a few cigarettes in it.
We were rewarded immediately with some fresh oranges. Of
course, we were soon copied and more fruit was being unloaded by this bartering than was going into the hold. The
announcement came threatening court martial if anyone was
caught. Ah well, I recalled the words of my old Seaforth
Highlander sergeant in training at Glasgow, "Every man is
born with a certain amount of natural cunning – it is up to
you to develop it in the Army!"

The next morning we were in the Red Sea. It was like a
huge mirror stretching in every direction with scarcely a ripple

on the water. The land was a reddish, burnt colour and barren of vegetation. The ship made good time in this sea but it was very hot and men were being sunburned despite warnings of the dangers. Soon we entered the harbour of Aden to refuel and take on more supplies. Small boys were diving for coins, mostly silver sixpences. They would not dive for a copper penny. Some smart guys would cover a penny with silver paper and throw it overboard. The young boys just grinned – this had been done before.

In the middle of the harbour was a small structure on a rock. This was a leper colony and inmates were clearly visible as they limped around the building. Some of the ship's crew had a swim off the stern of the ship. This ended abruptly when an Arab began yelling and splashing the water; a shark had been spotted and the crew beat a hasty retreat up the anchor chain. The show was over.

Before leaving Aden we were assembled at our boat stations and stood to attention. Apparently a Royal Navy destroyer was leaving Aden with a high ranking naval officer on board. He was probably down in the mess swilling down rum for all we knew or cared. We were not impressed by this "bull". Life was hard enough without this nonsense.

We soon left Aden and formed a somewhat smaller convoy with escorts from the Indian Navy. Our destination could be Bombay, Madras or Australia. Checks on the sun soon indicated Bombay, which was the most logical choice. The Indian Ocean was calm and pleasant. The troops organized a deck concert and talent competition. They had acquired the use of a large piano and were manoeuvring it along the deck. Among the volunteers was a big, thin soldier who invariably carried a Bible in his hand. He was very religious and self-righteous. As they heaved and strained over the large piano in a poorly co-ordinated manner, one small lad accidentally pushed the wrong way and bruised the toe of the lad with the Bible. He yelled loudly in pain and screamed at the small lad, slapping him with his hand and exclaimed, "Pestilence upon you!" I thought then that this was the best act of the concert. The contestants sang dirty songs, told jokes, played harmonicas etc. The clear winner was a lad from Skye who sang in both Gaelic and English and also explained the meaning of the traditional Gaelic song. I guess the men were in reality more susceptible to his message.

The voyage to Bombay was uneventful and we arrived early one morning at Bombay anchorage which was full of ships of all types and sizes. It was the main supply line to our forces at Burma at this time. Everyone was preparing to disembark except our unit which intrigued us. We were quickly taken onto the dockside and told we had leave for four hours when we must be back by 6 pm on board the ship. Of course no reasons were given. We formed up on the dock in three ranks and our Regimental Sergeant Major gave us a pep talk. He pointed out that the locals were quite different from us – for which no doubt they were extremely grateful! We must not insult them or injure them. We must not visit the native quarters – as far as we could see it was all native quarters. We were to be aware of pickpockets and prostitutes, most of whom would be certified virgins.

We were finally let loose on India. We had in our gang an old soldier who had served in India in peacetime so we felt we would be well guided. At the dock gate there was a merchant with a hand cart filled with oranges built into a pyramid. Since we had not seen oranges at home for years we gathered round to buy some. However, our old soldier,

Mitchell, announced that we need not buy them. He picked up the orange at the peak of the pyramid and under close scrutiny of the vendor he threw it to the next man and said, "Play donkey", where the orange travelled in a circle still under the watchful eye of the vendor. As it went its rounds Mitchell removed an orange for each of us into his tunic. He then calmly returned the passing orange to the vendor and left. I felt ashamed and gave the Indian two rupees, much to the disgust of Mitchell. Eventually I would come to appreciate the kindness of the Indian soldier.

Our visit to Bombay was a let down as the out of bounds quarter was the only place where most of the men wanted to visit. There was so much of historical importance to see in Bombay. However, as we had not had a decent meal on the ship we visited a nice restaurant and I ordered a large slice of bacon surrounded by small fried eggs on a large oval platter. I can't believe I ate the whole thing!

On return to the ship we were told to be ready to disembark after breakfast the next morning. This meant one thing, we would probably be going on a long journey by train – hence the shore leave. Next morning we were loaded into army trucks and taken to a nearby railway station in the suburbs of Bombay. Here we waited for hours amid large tenement-type buildings where the locals obviously lived. We noticed Indians walking over the open ground with a small brass bowl in their hand. The squatted down on their heels and defecated then washed their rear ends with water from the brass bowl. No wonder the place stank, yet I believe these homes must have had Asian toilets.

When our troop train arrived it was so dirty and infested with cockroaches we had to clean the carriages before we could board it. The windows operated like the old fashioned shutters of a tram car by pulling a leather strap to close them. We slept on the benches and also on the racks above. We had strict instructions to guard our rifles as they could be stolen and end up on the Northwest Frontier. The carriages had running boards and as we crawled slowly out of the city, numerous vendors jumped on and tried to sell us anything from genuine gold rings to flick knives. One Sikh was particularly troublesome as he kept flicking his knife in front of us. Our old soldier Mitchell cured him. He had one lad pull the strap and trap the vendor's hands inside while he relieved him of the knife and all his rings, much to his annoyance. The last we saw of him he was jumping up and down by the track and mixing Indian and English insults at us.

The abject poverty all around us was very disturbing to me as I had been raised in poverty but nothing to the extent of the squalor I was seeing. I was, in a way, ashamed to be white.

Our carriageway was uncomfortable but no worse than the troop ship. Our toilets were Asian and consisted of a hole in the floor with two places for your feet on each side of it. Above hung two rings which supported you while you attempted to defecate Asian style. It was a culture shock. Toilet paper was of course not supplied, although the British army must have travelled in India for about 100 years.

We were aware the next morning that the rear of the train contained another unit from West Africa. They were Negro soldiers with white NCOs and officers. They caused great amusement. They received their rations each morning and they promptly ate the lot at one go, then came begging from us when the train stopped, which was very frequently, at small stations and sometimes in the middle of nowhere. These men wore their army boots around their neck and never seemed to remove their webbing equipment. At one stage when we were crossing the great Decan Plateau of India we stopped in the middle of nowhere for about two hours.

During this time one of our men got down on the track and in boredom started throwing rocks from the track at a post in the middle of a large pond. Within minutes the whole West African unit was out throwing rocks and the track was rapidly being denuded of stones. They seemed to mimic everything we did. Finally their NCO ordered them back on board the train. As he passed by he grinned at us and said, "They are right out of the trees you know." They also soon copied the Indian beggars and came limping along with their outstretched hand and a big grin. Much later I was to discover that they did very well against the Japanese in the Burmese jungle except for occasions when they were mortared or could not see where the fire was coming from. They thought it was magic and took off out of the way.

After a few days of very slow progress we arrived at a small station, where much to our delight we were allowed to disembark and were given our first cooked meal since leaving the troop ship. There were a few white women there to supervise, obviously colonial types but very polite and friendly. A big sign overhead read, "Welcome 14th Army". There was no doubt now that we were headed to Calcutta! Why the army found it necessary to keep this secret was beyond comprehension.

After five days on the troop train we were glad to get off at Calcutta. At that station we struggled with all our kit and rifles as we negotiated the throng of natives on the platforms.

When we inquired, "Why the mob?" we were told they come here to sleep at night as they have nowhere else to go.

Our journey by truck to our transit camp was also an eye opener. The squalor was appalling and everywhere. The transit camp was very orderly and clean. Anything that moved you saluted and if it did not move it was painted white. Life was not too bad here, food was good and the wooden Indian beds with string mattresses called charpoies were comfortable. Our RSM gave us a big lecture on security. He warned us that "loose wallahs" or thieves were so adept they could come in the night and tickle you to make you turn over in bed, then remove your wallet from beneath you. Ironically, the only man to lose his wallet there was the RSM. We all laughed at this but the net result was a doubling of the guard and that meant duty for us. We ate in the mess hall which was simply a bamboo roof on large wooden pillars with army tables and benches. We collected our food from a nearby army field kitchen and walked to the mess hall.

In India there are large crow-like brown birds called kites which are acrobatic flyers and great scavengers. They were affectionately called shite-hawks by the troops. They could relieve you of any choice morsel on your dinner plate in one silent swoop. Cheese seemed to be their favourite. It was a common army joke that when the food was poor, the shite-hawks would not even bother to swoop on it, they would sit up in the trees and say, "Not that garbage again."

Our camp was adjacent to a Hindu burial place. Small slender Indians would arrive regularly carrying a rough bamboo stretcher with a corpse for disposal. They jogged along with their load and if it tipped off they quickly retrieved it and proceeded on their way. These bodies were burned in an open fire on a platform and the smell of burning flesh was every-where. At times the attendants would give out a yell and strike the skull of the burning carcass. This was another culture shock.

We were allowed a trip into the city which was quite an experience. Small single-deck tram cars travelled the various city routes. It was noticeable that more passengers travelled on top of the carriages than inside, the reason being on the roof was free. Stops were made for cows while they wandered over the tracks. The cow is, of course, sacred and must never be harmed. They served no purpose other than as religious sym-bols, although their dung was collected, dried and made into patties which were used as fuel for cooking or heating by the natives.

Oxen were the only means of traction for ploughing, cul-tivation and transport and caused a serious problem in traffic which was always heavy on the main streets. It seemed that every driver blew his horn incessantly which means that the horn lost all its purpose as a means of warning. Our RSM would lean out over the front of our 15-cwt truck and whack the natives with his long stick to exhort them to move out of the way, all the while questioning their parentage or inquiring if their father was a monkey. It was a case of, do as I say – not do as I do. We were also warned that some natives would deliberately acquire injuries to obtain compensation from the army. I suppose this was preferable to the abject poverty with no hope of improvement in their lot. It seemed a very ill-di-vided world.

The short time in the transit camp did allow us to talk with men from other units, some of which had been up in the forward areas in Burma and were here to rest and recuperate. There was of course no front line in Burma, merely a forward area of dense jungle-clad mountains severed by deep river valleys. The Japanese forward area and ours could often cover miles of the same territory, such were the conditions where the war in Burma was fought. I recall lying one night on the warm ground in a camp, chatting to a young soldier returned with his unit. He painted a grim picture and also lost two of his best mates, killed by the Nips as they were often called. This derivation is from Sons of Nippon (Japan).

Up to then, the war had been, in a sense, a game to someone of my age. Suddenly it was a deadly game and one which would become even more deadly. I did two useful things while in Calcutta. I bought a book on Urdu, the Indian language used by the Indian army and also a map of India and Burma. These two purchases were to prove most useful to me in the years to come.

After about a week in the transit camp we prepared to move out by train. Again it was the same deal in a small dirty train with Asian toilets. However, we knew from my map that this journey would not be too long. We headed through Bengal Province then towards Assam. We finally disembarked at a small railway station in the middle of nowhere called Panagarh in Burdwan Province. Army trucks ferried us to our new camp – and what a camp! It reminded me of films of the Foreign Legion. There was a circle of rough stone huts with bamboo roofs and windows with no glass and no doors, only entrances. There were some brick washrooms with showers and toilets close by. The huts had the usual charpois beds and blankets but no pillows. Mosquito nets were provided over each bed. The cook-house was a few hundred yards away and the mess hall was in the open. As far as the eye could see there were desolate, barren, sandy fields, which had already been subdivided and cultivated Indian style at one time. I believe the lack of habitation was due to severe drought over a number of years.

The troops quickly adapted to this desolate, isolated camp and we wondered why we were here. We soon learned that a couple of miles away was a large army engineering depot where we would assist with the unloading of wagons and storing of all the engineering supplies needed by an army – portable prefabricated barracks from the USA, railway equipment, steel, cement, etc., etc.

We had numerous small slender Bengali coolies to unload the trucks. They spoke Bengali which was incomprehensible to me except for a few words like pani-wallah (water boy), utao (lift up) and jildi jao (hurry up). Their skill at removing huge wooden cases from deep sided wagons onto the railway side was remarkable. They used the Principle of Moments, i.e. levers, with dexterity and without the benefit of high school physics or mathematics. However they did stink due to the application of a mustard-like oil they rubbed on their bare bodies and hair. This combined with perspiration made them smell like pole-cats. To their fellow workers they smelled just fine. I once talked to an educated Bengali who informed me that we smelled just as noxious to them. He assured me this was not just a racial joke but was genuine. From a biological point of view this concept appears to be quite acceptable. We were poles apart racially, so why would our scent be similar.

I well remember one Englishman making fun of my Scottish accent. I informed him that an accent was a relative thing and his gibberish was just as peculiar to me. In any case, we had the language and he had the accent.

The days of work were tiresome under the Bengal sun as

we started work at 5.30 am and worked until 1.00 pm. On rest day my mate and I ventured over the plains with a stout stick in case we encountered snakes which were common in the area. We made our way to a small Hindu settlement, a few native huts or bashas around a large communal pond with places for washing clothes. We quickly noticed that the children were whisked inside the huts by their mothers and we were being monitored from behind the shutters. I was very brown from the sun and my mate was fairly white so I blamed it all on him. Probably most of these kids and women had never seen a white man. One small boy beside the water, banging clothes on a large stone which was the customary method of doing laundry, stared at us with wide eyes and obvious fear. I produced a bar of army emergency ration chocolate and gave him a piece to eat. He loved it and ran off home with the rest. I was sure that his first encounter with a white man would be remembered.

They work was boring and a complete waste of time and training. I asked to see my CO, an old colonel from World War I who had served in North Africa in the invasion of Morocco and Tunisia in the British 2nd Army. I explained that I had interrupted my university career to join the army. In reality I was too poor to return to my second year in engineering at Glasgow University. He was rude to me and said he doubted if any field engineers would have me. I said I had remembered most of my sapper training and was willing to test it against his choice of any other rank. He dismissed me from the office disdainfully. We did have one detachment in Calcutta docks and another near Chittagong. Within a few days, accompanied by a corporal, I was posted to join our detachment near Chittagong as a replacement. At last I was finally going to do something useful. The Colonel was a poor CO. He never said goodbye or wished us well. His only instructions were to see that our pay-books and wills were completed.

We had to go by rail back to Calcutta then by rail again to a port on the Brahmaputra River. Here we boarded an old Mississippi river boat with a large paddle wheel. We sailed down the enormous river, we could scarcely see the far bank, to another river port. Here we boarded a narrow gauge railway car for Chittagong. I remember the roof swayed side to side as we travelled along.

We soon discovered that the docks at Chittagong had been bombed by the Japanese. They swept in from the Bay of Bengal and dropped anti-personnel bombs on the docks. The poor native labour did not take cover but stood watching them and were cut to pieces in a terrible slaughter where they stood. The net result was that there was no native labour available for weeks. They had all taken off to the bush. An Indian Army Pioneer Corps was brought in to help us unload the supplies for the 14th Army in the Arakan region of Burma. I was soon with our own detachment stationed in tents near to a US Army Air Corps airfield south of Chittagong. We had one captain and eight men and we formed a very happy and active unit. The men were all much older than me at 19. The next oldest was 28 and the rest all in their thirties or even forties. I was also the only sapper among corporals, sergeants and warrant officers. I was subsequently called the "kid" much to my indignation. In spite of this I was determined never to show any outward sign of fear, it was a point of honour and my secret. Much later on I was busy deepening the ditch around our tents when from inside the tent I heard one man say, "That goddamned kid is not afraid of anything." I rubbed my hands with glee – my tactics had succeeded and I felt I was a big guy just like the old soldiers who were my mates.

We worked very hard, sometimes all night to get supplies loaded aboard the DC-3s which would deliver them to the troops in the jungle by parachute. At first we dealt with the US Air Force and we had a great rapport with them. Somehow the US forces wanted for nothing even in Burma. They gave us jungle blankets, chocolate, sweets, cigarettes, small insecticide bombs which killed the mosquitoes and bugs by the hundreds in our tents. They asked me one day if I had bed sheets and I just said, "What are they?" I was immediately given an olive-green nylon parachute to use as bed linen. One of the lads had acquired an Indian sari off a clothes line. He slept in this much to the ribald comments from his mates.

After some time the US Air Force, which was being replaced by the RAF, had a jeep in the bottom of the deep monsoon ditch where it was firmly stuck in the deep mud next to the air strip. No effort seemed to be made to retrieve it as it was thought to be impossible.

As soon as the Yanks left we had it out in no time using a Coles crane and our mechanic got it going and we set about cleaning it up. Then right there on the hood in white letters was "Commanding Officer". We threw more mud over it and hid it in a spare tent. We had our own jeep which was a godsend to us. We could get to various units and scrounge anything we badly needed. Alas, our captain was a real jerk and he decided that would be *his* jeep; a most arrogant man.

Our mechanic was not amused and suddenly the jeep was no longer running. Our captain, who was supposed to be an engineer officer, berated this poor man and ordered him to get that jeep running. Our mechanic gave him a line of technical "bull" as to why it would not run and which new spares it needed. Our captain had obviously only a nodding acquaintance with the workings of an internal combustion engine and was powerless to refute the mechanic's opinion.

Fortunately the captain was soon replaced by a lieutenant who was easy going and I suspect congenitally pissed, as he was definitely upper crust. He was invariably full of gin or Rosa rum. We explained to him that this jeep was really ours but he could use it if he wished. Within minutes of his reply, "That would be OK boys," the jeep was running perfectly. We were even allowed a ration of petrol for it but, of course, the Army issued a form to record the mileage every week and that was rationed too. When we exceeded our limit I had the bright idea of placing the form in the mud and running the wheel over it just once then drying it and explaining to the officer what had happened. It worked! So much for army regulations. The time we had the jeep was certainly an easier life than before its acquisition.

The time soon arrived for us to move on to a very different function. We were to be used to support various Indian and Gurkha units with our engineering skills. The Indian Army had a few engineer units of their own but the task of handling mines, booby-traps and explosives was to be allocated to us as support troops.

By now, in 1944, the Japanese were being beaten at their own game and were opposed by at least equal strength of Allied troops and equipment. In fact the tables were now turned and the little yellow Sons of Heaven were being pushed southward almost everywhere. As the Japs left they mined the roads and jungle tracks, set booby-traps and poisoned the village wells to deny us clean fresh water. They blew small bridges as they went south.

In a land like Burma there were countless rivers, streams and creeks which had to be bridged to allow army traffic to move. Although timber was available everywhere, the Bailey bridge was by far the easiest, fastest and best way to bridge even gaps of ten to fifteen feet. All these Bailey panels and transoms had to be brought up by road for this purpose. It was a long tedious task especially when you knew that down the track a little more, bridges of all sizes were required. From the bridging of the huge Chindwin and Irrawadi rivers to the small streams and creeks, the Bailey bridge proved to be a decisive factor in the success against the Japanese armies. They were easy to maintain and very dependable. Their heaviest load would be a 40-ton Sherman tank but generally 25-pounder field guns and 3-ton trucks were the normal load carried. After a short time you could become very adept at their construction, unlike in the days of training.

The work on explosives was much more demanding and dangerous. Generally the Nips laid their mines on a track or road, since in Burma progress at a reasonable rate was only possible on those routes. Invariably, mines were set in an obvious place in a clear area of a track. You could be sure that Japanese snipers were positioned in trees to take out the sappers as they worked to defuse them. Infantry men were deployed to protect you on this job which was at least some comfort. If the Gurkhas had the job to protect you your confidence was greatly increased as they would personally track down any Nip if he fired on you and bring you his severed bloody head as a friendly gesture.

The Gurkha was a heroic little soldier in whom you could

have complete trust with your life. I recall visiting the Burma Star Reunion in the Albert Hall, London, after the war and the Gurkha Pipes and Drums were marched into the arena. I had a distinct lump in my throat at the sight of these men who were probably the sons of the Gurkha who had served me so well. The recollections of war are both sad and amusing. We tend to remember the pleasant ones but in reality the sad memories lie deep but nevertheless easily remembered on occasion.

The time had come to say goodbye to our American Air Corps friends. They were being moved with all their DC-3 Dakota transport aircraft to northeast Burma to support General Stillwell, the US Commander, affectionately known as "Vinegar Joe", because of his sour relations with his allies. They were to depart with a full load of stores and equipment which had to be on the air strip and loaded for take-off by 0800 hours the next day.

We toiled all day and night to assemble these supplies but as the time drew near the Yanks were all sitting around shooting dice and gambling. I should point out that in this forlorn place, cash was of little use as there was nothing to buy. I had just indicated to my RSM that our work was completed in haste for nothing, when a jeep drove on to the airstrip and the US Commandant leapt out and shouted, "Come on fellas." At once everyone was working including the CO and his entourage and the lead plan taxied down the runway right on 0800 hours. This was a lesson in "American get up and go" and one from which our officer could have benefited. Needless to say he had still not surfaced.

We waved goodbye to our friends who had treated us so well. The RAF soon took over and we still worked with them in the same manner except everything had to be weighed before loading. As the war progressed and the Japanese were driven south our function was over and we were ordered to move south by air. This means we had to persuade the RAF to take our pride and joy, our jeep. They firmly refused. We tried everything we could, even bribery, but to no avail. In desperation we decided to sell it, but to whom?

An Indian officer offered to take it but of course had little money which was of little immediate use anyway. The final price after much negotiation, Indian bargaining genes against Scottish, was a bottle of Johny Walker whisky. Ah well, it was the best deal we could make. We could have given it to the RAF – NO WAY!

My job, being the "kid" of the group, was to divide up the whisky into eight portions. I remember well those eight olive-green metal mugs lined up in a row, while I carefully tried to dispense one-eight of a jeep-worth into each.

Prepared to leave by DC-3 about 5am we slept under mosquito nets beneath the wing until first light when a RAF jeep almost ran over us. The RAF administration type gave us hell for being in the way. My big rough mate from London informed him we had been there all night unlike him. I could not help comparing him to the US Commanding Officer. However, once aboard the crew were very apologetic for their desk-bound colleague.

We still had no idea where we were going, but it was obviously south and east. The Burmese jungle is quite a sight from the air, endless miles of jungle covered hills with deep ravines. We actually flew over a huge floating Bailey Bridge for which we had supplied the parts. It may have been over the Chindwin river or the Irrawadi river.

Most of the time we lay on the sloping floor of the plane under our jungle blanket. It was really pleasant to feel cool again. We had to remain fairly still as we had no oxygen and we were about 10,000 feet up. There was no door on the aircraft, just a small piece of rope across a gap on the fuselage of about four feet square where supplies were dropped out and parachuted to the troops below.

After some time I moved to the tail where there was a small toilet behind a door. After finishing my visit I got up to open the door and discovered that my mates were gone and there was not a sound. The plane was flying normally so I clambered up the slippery sloping floor to the cabin behind a bulkhead. They were all squeezed in there and laughing and grinning at me. The pilot had brought them forward to keep his tail up for landing on a rough strip up ahead in a clearing in the jungle. The pilot had scared me as I emerged from the toilet as he was banking steeply and I was gazing down through the open hole in the fuselage. I asked him why he was banking and he casually replied he was looking to see who was in possession of the strip. By now I regarded this as a move to scare me but he was indeed serious.

We were ordered to throw everything out as soon as he landed and run quickly to the bush at the perimeter of the field. As soon as this was accomplished he rapidly turned the aircraft around and took off again for home base. We obeyed his orders and recovered the rest of the cargo later. We soon knew the reason for our presence. There was a Japanese bunker on a hillside at one end of the airstrip. Obviously it was still occupied by Nips and was a real nuisance to our aircraft. Our job would be so neutralize it but not till we had appraised the situation carefully.

The Japanese bunker was a formidable obstruction. It was holed out of a hillside and tree trunks were piled against the opening of the tunnel. Earth was piled over the timbers and a small orifice was left for the Japanese 75-millimetre gun and small arms. The hillside was protected by mines and booby-traps and of course the whole field of fire was carefully laid out. It was difficult to get near it and only a direct hit could take it out.

The tunnel into the hillside was deep and full of ammunition and provisions. The defenders were invariably suicide squads. It was not a very attractive proposition to have to neutralize this type of strong point. Obviously the artillery had tried to reduce it and even Hurri bombers and Hurricane fighter aircraft with cannon could not demolish it. The Nips had the range down to a tee for almost every location on the field and could blast a DC-3 when it landed if they felt like it.

We trudged a couple of miles to a nearby village beside the main road south where we met the local road marshal. He was the officer responsible for directing traffic on the road and ensuring that during darkness all troops and vehicles were in a harbour area overnight which was defended against attack. The Nips actually were in a state of chaos in 1945 as they were attempting to cross this road from west to east and regroup to fight their way towards Siam. They were in bad shape and short of everything thanks to the defeat inflicted on them by the 14th Army during the recent several months of continuous combat. They were also very desperate and dangerous.

We were allowed to sleep in the old Burmese schoolhouse, one of the wooden buildings sitting on large teak stilts which stood everywhere in this area of monsoon rains. At least we would be dry for the night and we settled down on the floor.

We were safe enough as we had Gurkha guards around the village. We had army hard tack rations but no drinking water. The Japanese had poisoned the local village well when they withdrew. They had used Paris green which contains arsenic. These were common tactics by the Japanese, but very effective in harassing the advancing troops.

My London mate and I decided to go in search of fresh water. I had passed a few Burmese huts on the way into the village and I was sure that they must have some water. We took a big army dixie which held about three gallons of water with ease, and some tea, sugar and condensed milk. We took also our rifles and bayonets and ammunition just in case for the Nips were everywhere in the hills nearby.

We reached a little square of native huts at the side of the road where an old Burmese lady was tending a wood fire. She had a tiny cute little Burmese child with her. As we approached she was scared. These poor people had suffered very badly at the hands of the Japs who took whatever they needed from them without a qualm. My mate, who was a big rough guy was a bit anxious and I had to tell him to cool it and take it easy or we would be out of luck altogether. By the fire I lifted the little child on my knee and got my mate to puncture a tin of condensed milk. I knew from my own childhood how sweet it was. I put some on my finger and fed it to the little boy. He loved it.

The old lady beamed and was obviously reassured. She then went off to a nearby hut and came back with another little child. I said to my mate, "This one's for you!" He took him on his knee and fed him in the same manner, only he spoke to him saying, "You slant-eyed little bastard, I bet your father was monkey." Needless to say he was at heart, a decent kind

chap for all his outward appearance. The mother and grand-
mother were of course delighted as they had no idea what was
being said. There was no doubt in their minds that we were
friendly and kind and could be trusted. I guess mothers everywhere would have reacted in the same way.

We slowly got around to the question of water to make tea.
Clean water was very scarce and had obviously been carried
on their heads for a long way from a spring. The old lady put
about half a gallon in the bottom of our dixie and my mate
began to swear. I cooled him off and told him to take it slowly.
I explained with the use of my fingers, we were eight men
and more. Reluctantly, she put in enough for everyone and
it was soon boiling. My mate threw in some loose tea then
he punctured a can of condensed milk and threw the whole
tin into the water. When the label floated off he removed it
and the tin with a stick. Our tea was ready and after thanking
the ladies we headed for our mates.

Our useless officer immediately enquired if it was safe and
I said, "Watch me sir," as I scooped up a mug of hot tea and
drank it. He enquired where we got the water and I said from
a local spring known to the villagers. Everyone drank their fill
and the RSM complimented me. My officer said, "Oh yes,
intrepid chaps!" I could not print my mate's response to this
but it concerned his rear end.

We ate our hard tack rations, then settled down for a nice
sleep on a dry floor. However, that was not to be. As it was
getting dark the building on stilts was rocked by repeated
bangs, obviously 25-pounder guns of an Indian field regiment
nearby. We cursed them, but as often happens, we had reason
to be grateful for them. It seemed that this bunker had become
a real pain in the neck to the operation of this badly-needed

airstrip and the Indian gunners had been brought up to have another go at it. They had ranged it in daylight and as soon as it became dusk they opened up on it with a vengeance. Next day we were glad to learn that it had sustained a direct hit and was apparently neutralized. There was now no need to climb up there and deliver a pole charge into the opening. A 25-pound shell had dropped right in it and saved us the trouble.

It was a few days before we were sent up to ensure it was neutralized completely. Even this would be a risky job as it was probably mined around the approaches. After a few days we ventured up and removed any charges and trip wires on the hillside. The bunker had a Japanese 75 gun and machine-gun which had almost been buried by the roof falling in on it after being hit by a shell. There was a great heap of soil with the brown leather boots of a Japanese officer sticking out of the heap. The place was beginning to stink with the heat and the decaying flesh. We found the inside of the tunnel was still intact and all kinds of provisions, rice, tins of fish, clean clothes, water and, of course, ammunition was piled in the very rear of the tunnel. Two Japanese officers were the only occupants and they were both dead.

We decide to just seal it all off and placed charges near the entrance with long fuses. It all caved in nicely. As far as I know these Nips still lie there where they fought. This was a very common occurrence in Burma. Often men were never found. Indeed, according to military records, the Burma campaign was the longest campaign of World War II and also had the highest percentage of "missing in action".

We had some difficulty before closing the bunker off with explosives. In our group was a soldier who had been out in the Far East for over three years and he had seen a great deal of action. So much so that his mind was definitely affected. He collected souvenirs from the Japanese, mainly gold teeth which he kicked from their heads before burial. These teeth he kept in a large red cloth like a handkerchief and he would sit sometimes and lay them all out in a row and count them. Some of his mates used to tease him that he had lost some and this made him do endless recounts. His repatriation was long overdue! When he saw the Japanese officers leather boots sticking out of the heap he immediately said, "Oh boy, souvenirs." The place stank of death which was fairly common when a body lies in the tropical heat in Burma. Needless to say we ejected him from the bunker then blew it up.

Our job was completed there and we were to move on to a Gurkha unit for further duty, still unknown. I think the worst part of active service in our small group was the complete lack of communications from above. We seldom were briefed before moving and consequently often went unprepared for our task. Our officer could not have run a Christmas club in civilian life. Thank God we had a very good warrant officer. At least we usually managed to determine roughly where we were in Burma, which was very helpful if we were cut off from our forces and had to find our way back. Such circumstances were not uncommon in Burma, where our forward area often overlapped with the Japanese forward area and of course jungle covered hills and villages can all look alike even when you can get up high enough to have a look around.

After a few miles marching along a main road we arrived at the Gurkha unit and reported for duty. It was always a great feeling for me to be with these brave little soldiers. We never needed to worry about Japanese infiltration when we were with them, but the Japanese did, as they were adept at going out and bringing in a few Nips dead or alive.

We were to assist them with mines, demolitions and booby-traps. I was sent to report to their CO, a major of the British army. The Nips had placed a mine on a track which was the usual site for such a weapon as almost all movement was along tracks in the dense jungle. As suspected this mine was set in the middle of the track but in an area which allowed full sighting of anyone sent to disarm it. The Nips generally had snipers up high in trees awaiting our attempts at neutralizing mines. At times they would set up a trip-wire across the path or between trees which would trip a booby-trap, generally a charge attached to a pull igniter so if you spotted the booby-trap you could still get a sniper's bullet through your head. The Gurkhas were on detail to protect. It was a point of honour to protect their man and they took this very seriously. I met a few men who owed them their lives and many wounded whom they rescued.

I reported to the Major who was standing with another officer surveying the track. He looked me up and down and said, "But you are just a kid, fancy sending a kid to do our dirty work."

I immediately replied, "I can do the job, sir." My voice betrayed my indignation. I hated to be called a kid, thinking I was a really big guy and equal to my much older mates.

The Major pointed out the position and detailed some Gurkhas to protect me. He cautioned me to be careful and again, I assured him I could do it. He walked away shaking his head and muttering to his fellow officer, "Just a kid."

The mine was not booby-trapped as far as I could see and it was probably hastily laid in position with not much attempt to conceal it. I had, however, been trained to avoid being deceived in this manner. Often a second pull igniter could be attached to it underneath. I made my careful examination before attempting to move it. I disarmed it and removed the fuse then carefully lifted the mine out of its hole.

The job was done and I walked up to the Major and handed him the fuse. He pulled away and said, "I believe you, just dispose of it in your usual way." He then thanked me and I was dismissed. I was anxious to rejoin my mates to see if they still called me "the kid" – they did, much to my annoyance.

We spent a few days in this position awaiting the Japanese who were supposed to be trying to cross the man road and move east towards Siam. They had been using trails through the jungle all the way from Arakan in the west of Burma. All routes had been cut north to south and this was their only way out of Burma to reach their main forces further east. The Gurkhas kept coming to us and asking for detonating fuse. This was in fact FID which meant fuse instantaneous detonating in army language. It detonated with a sharp crack at a rate of ninety feet per second and could be used as a "neclace" to cut a small tree trunk of up to about four inches in diameter. We supplied them with this fuse as we had lots available but we wondered why they wanted it. We reckoned it was just for fun and we would let them have it without question.

At this time the Japanese were sending out patrols to determine our position and strength and which troops were facing them. They had in the past removed Sikhs who never cut their hair but wrap it up in a turban as part of their religion. The Nips would cut all their hair off then beat them up before returning them to our lines. This was designed to demoralize the Sikh's unit and it was generally successful.

A Japanese is quite prepared to die in battle but his religion and custom required a sample of his hair or finger nails to be sent back to his relatives to be enshrined. The Japanese I knew had small a leather pouch on their belt which contained this type of memento and they were terrified if you wanted to remove it.

The Gurkhas were playing the Japanese at their own game. They would sneak out and grab a couple of Japanese and wrap this FID around their necks and blow their heads off. They would return the rest for the Japanese to find. This of course upset them as they do not like the head removed from the body making identification difficult. One day the Gurkhas came to us with a wicker basket with fish in it. We thought they had been fishing with explosives and were giving us some of their catch in return for the FID. We soon suspected there was some other reason for their big friendly grin on their faces. Two bloody Japanese heads lay beneath the fish. This was Gurkha humour and we could not avoid a good laugh at this bizarre incident. We were good friends.

The Gurkha soldier always carried his traditional weapon, his *kukri*, a short curved sword which he kept incredibly sharp. Before returning it to his scabbard he would draw blood by nicking his finger to maintain his ritual. I remember being shown the different slashing strokes performed in butchering their enemies. They always finished by removing the head – hence the Japanese fear of these brave little loyal soldiers.

When I eventually reached Rangoon a Burmese told me that when the Japanese first took Rangoon they had only one question of the locals – *Doko chisia* Indian – which simply asked, where are the small Indians? They meant of course the Gurkhas for whom they had a healthy respect.

Many years after the war I visited Katmandu in Nepal where I saw the Gurkhas in training at their depot. I had a lump in my throat which became noticeable to our local Nepalese guide. He escorted me towards the officer in charge and obviously explained my sentiments. He shook my hand then called his men to attention in Gurkali, their language. He told them I was ex-14th Army. They gave me a hearty cheer which really choked me up completely. I was not part of the Forgotten Army here, at least the Nepalese knew all about us, as well they might. Many Gurkhas died or were wounded in action in the 14th Army in Burma – probably the fathers of these men. It was a momentous occasion for me and one I will always remember.

The few days I spent with this Gurkha unit soon came to an end but rather unpleasantly. The Major whom I had en-countered over the land-mine was killed. The Nips had brought up some 75-millimetre field guns and had fired a few rounds at our position. Generally the Nips always seemed to fire four shells, one after the other – one in front, one behind, then get out as the next two were right on you. They did the same with mortars but they were even more accurate. Unfortunately, this officer got a shell all to himself and was killed. He was a good officer and it was a great shock. The worst part was my mate and I were told to dig his grave. We did this next to the track where it would be easily found later by the War Graves Commission, making sure it was deep enough, as we often found piards (wild dogs) which came in packs and searched for bodies. We wrapped him up in a jungle blanket, we did not have body bags then, laid him to rest and filled in the grave. I made a rough cross with two branches and I tied the cross with a spare boot-lace I had kept. It was a rough job done with my sapper's jack-knife. I hung his hat on the cross and the job was complete. My heart was heavy as this man had been so considerate of me, the "kid". It was the irony of war, but still tough to take.

Almost at once we heard a rumble. Gurkha patrols went out ahead of us, then the Major's whole unit arrived for his burial. The Last Post sounded then three shots over the grave by a firing party. It was all over and the Gurkhas withdrew. I sat by the cross for some time remembering the man who had been so concerned for my safety as a young soldier. Finally, I felt the firm hand of my warrant officer on my shoulder. He merely said, "Come on, Kid, it is over," he understood my feelings. It was a sad farewell to the Gurkhas.

Our work with the Gurkhas was soon completed and we were on the move again to another unit. The worst part of service in the jungle was the lack of information. We were a small unit of eight men and an officer going from unit to unit. These were always Indian units and the opportunity to gain up-to-date information was very limited. We had no idea of the general course of the war in Burma, except we knew that we were advancing and when we were withdrawing. At least in the 8th Army in Libya troops knew pretty well how the campaign was going and who were opposing them.

Life in the jungle could be very uncomfortable even when there was no fighting. Everything was soaking wet and it was very humid by night and day, but especially in the tropical sun. Our biggest discomfort was from skin disease. Most men who had to march through the jungle had skin diseases on their feet, crotch, armpits, waists, etc.

Tinea, or foot-rot, was the most unpleasant skin disease. The fungus thrived between the toes and caused terrible irritation which progressed to weeping sores and more irritation. If you got this infection on your crotch or armpits it made marching very uncomfortable. One of my mates had it very badly in his crotch. We got to a field ambulance and he received treatment which I believe was Castellani's paint, a medication introduced by the Italians for their soldiers during their invasion of Ethiopia. In a first aid tent a tall Sikh orderly was trying to paint the crotch of my mate from behind. Of course it stung sharply and he jumped forward doubled over. The orderly pursued him diligently yelling for him to baito, which means stop. All around the tent he pursued him to complete his task. It was quite a pantomime. I could have sold tickets for the show.

Besides tinea infection we nearly all suffered from 'prickly heat'. This was a fine rash which occurred almost everywhere but usually over your back where you could not scratch it. It was non-infectious and due to sweating salt and high temperatures and humidity. Other attacks on your skin came from mosquito bites which could be quite itchy if you scratched them.

In Burma there were all kinds of leeches. Generally, they were quite small and thin, like a small piece of thin string about one inch long. These creatures lived on leaves and awaited the passing of a warm blooded animal. They could sense the approach of a soldier and became active and ready to hook on their prey. Their presence could sometimes be sensed on a bush by a slight ripple of the leaves if they were in large numbers. They could quickly embed their mouth parts in the flesh and suck the blood. They became greatly enlarged and inflated with blood in a very short time. On no account should they be pulled off the skin. The head would be left in the flesh and a nasty infected wound would result. The trick was to burn their backsides with a lighted cigarette which causes them to drop off and often explode so that the ingested blood soiled clothing. I was a nonsmoker and had to make a quick dash to someone with a cigarette when attacked. Being a nonsmoker I was very popular with my mates, as I gave them my meagre cigarette ration routinely. They repaid me several times by killing my leeches. To this day I still have two scars on my legs to remind me of these horrible little bloodsuckers.

In some areas of Burma we were exposed to a water-borne parasite which completed its life cycle in snails. This parasite was similar to the liver flukes which often parasitize cattle and sheep. These are trematodes which have a similar life cycle in snails and water. The type found in Burma caused schistosomiasis and unlike the cattle variety (faseioliasis) it infected humans via water causing serious illness and even blindness. In addition other water-borne diseases posed a danger. Leptospirosis which causes nephritis and jaundice in domestic animals, especially dogs, was found in some areas and was certainly a problem in the Malayan jungle after the war.

Besides the skin diseases and water borne diseases there were several prevalent systemic diseases such as malaria, dengue fever, cholera, typhoid, typhus and various forms of dysentery. Then, of course, there was the most common disease – fever NYD which was diagnosed routinely and meaning, fever not yet diagnosed. At a field ambulance, which was the nearest first aid station in the forward area, this was standard practice. The MO generally became very adept at giving treatment to cover the likely cause of the fever.

I remember well when I was attached to an Indian army engineering unit, I had a terrible bout of dysentery. I had been friendly with a little Indian soldier who sat cross-legged by an open fire and made chapattis for his unit. These are round flat doughy things like pancakes, but very bland and filling. The Indians eat them with their rice as a staple diet much like we eat bread. This little Indian was a happy little soldier and sang as he made the chapattis between his palms then tossed them in the fire. I swear he could pull them out of the fire with his toes. I often sat beside him and chatted as best I could in broken Urdu, the Indian Army language and pigeon English.

When I was laid low with dysentery I lay on my army ground sheet in a little bivouac under a tree. My little Indian friend visited me regularly throughout the day and the night, bringing me strong stewed tea with lots of *chini* (sugar) and goat's milk. This unit had their own goats. He also made me a special chapatti with sugar in it to help my digestion. I know he kept me from being dehydrated from constant diarrhoea and I recovered after a few days, much to his delight. It was difficult to say if the pills I swallowed or his treatment cured me but nevertheless I forged a strong bond with my little Indian friend.

It was not uncommon for a small unit like mine to become very close to our parent Indian unit. There was a bond formed which was very strong. The bond formed between coal miners exposed constantly to danger was probably the only analogous association found in civilian life. This type of bond had no racial barriers.

The 14th Army in the beginning of the Burma campaign had many more casualties from malaria than from conflict, something like 100,000 men were laid low by malaria in the initial stages of the struggle. Fortunately Mepacrine tablets were introduced and we swallowed one per day to suppress, but not

cure or prevent malaria. These were aspirin-size yellow pills
which tasted horrible. The use of these pills was mandatory
every day. If you caught malaria you were automatically on a
charge for disobeying orders. As is often the case, men are
suspicious of such pills. Rumours went around that they made
you sterile. Of all the things, the thought of sterility had the
greatest impact since some of these men were away from home
for three to five years. The thought of not being able to
"perform" was a serious threat to morale. I was always amazed
at the toffee-nosed types at the War Office who did not
comprehend the fears and worries of men deprived of their
family life for such long periods. You can harangue, threaten
and order them all you like but you cannot forbid them to
worry.

Besides, the constant exposure to all forms of infectious
disease, we had the continual threat of snake bite. There were
snakes of all types and sizes in Burma. The krate was probably
the most dangerous as it was very poisonous and difficult to
see in the jungle. There was always the danger you would
step on one or contact one in the undergrowth. The banded
krate was easier to see as it had yellow bands all along its length
which was three to five feet. It was also deadly poisonous.
There was, in addition, the cobra, usually found in drier areas
where there were rats, on which they mainly lived.

I had a very narrow escape near the end of the war not far
from Rangoon. We had occupied the remnants of a building
which consisted of a high roof and wooden pillars every ten
feet or so. We wrapped hessian around the pillars to form walls
and keep out the rain. I had a little army table and a canvas
chair for an office and was seated there with my legs crossed
and my right foot rocking up and down. Suddenly an Indian

soldier behind me pulled me backwards, shouting "big snake, sahib." It was a close shave as the snake was watching the rhythmical movements of my boot, the way they will watch anything that oscillates or sways regularly. All I saw of the viper was its tail end as it retreated out under the canvas wall into a monsoon ditch. It was fairly dark in colour and obviously a big, deadly poisonous cobra. Once more I was indebted to an Indian!

There was also a small greenish snake which was only about one to two feet long and quite slender. Some of the troops called them mambas but these do not exist in Burma. Most of us referred to them as jungle snakes. They were extremely fast along the ground and also very poisonous. Fortunately, they were timid.

Life in the jungle was quite stressful but there were several precautions. Hygiene was all important as were clean dry feet. Dry socks were essential. An army marches on its feet and nowhere more than in the jungle. Despite Mepacrine tablets for malaria, protection from the mosquitoes by clothing and mosquito nets was essential. Drinking water, generally chlorinated, was awful to the taste. Boiling it well to make tea did help and made it safe. Drinking untreated water was an invitation to the hospital. Fresh drinking water was carried in large tanks by mules. Two tanks to a mule to balance the load. On many occasions water was flown in to airstrips in the jungle or even dropped by parachute to the troops in a jungle clearing.

Being with all Indian units we had usually only Indian rations. Rice twice a day with some liquid butter spread on it and of course chapattis. We had sometimes army hard tack or American K rations. The latter were very good. The British fourteen-man pack was meant for fourteen men for one day or, alternatively, one man for fourteen days and was mainly hard army biscuits and tinned food. The bully beef was good but often it was replaced by Australian corned mutton which was almost inedible and came out of the tin as a semi-liquid. It was full of mutton fat and was revolting. There was a story that one unit was mortaring the Nips but could not wipe them out of a position. They fired a tin of corned mutton at them saying, "If that last bomb didn't get you, this stuff will kill you!"

Indians, many of whom are Hindus, do not eat meat, especially beef. Nor do the Gurkhas. Moslem soldiers, of course, can eat meat but not pork. Hence in Indian units there was often no meat ration at all. British troops needed meat at least twice per week. Most of the time we were out of luck unless we got near British troops when we scrounged some rations from them. The fourteen-man packs did have bully beef and also treacle pudding which was very tasty and filling. The US K rations were just great, even scrambled egg and fried bacon, etc. Our own hard tack was very tasteless and dull. There were large slabs of thick heavy chocolate which was full of energy and vitamins but, as Crocodile Dundee would say, "It is good for you but tastes like shit." At times all our supplies came down by parachute, courtesy of the RAF or the US Air Corps. Even our olive-green toilet paper came down out of the sky. Many a time we watched and waited for our supplies and they nearly always arrived courtesy of these brave flyers who flew unarmed DC-3s across jungle clad mountains to find a small clearing in the jungle.

The air supply of an Indian division was of course much easier and less demanding than for a British division. Everything came out of the sky from food to water and ammunition.

Often after a drop we would root around to see if any British rations had been supplied, especially bread and bully beef. We were seldom lucky. Our greatest joy was getting to a US airstrip where our American friends could not do enough for us. Even their medical officer, if available, would gladly give us any treatment for disease or wounds we required. My praise for the Americans in Burma can never be too high. Our relations with them were more than friendly.

The American serviceman in the UK was well fed, well clothed and well paid and of course resented by his British counterpart. They used to say in the UK, they were overfed, overpaid, oversexed and over here. However in Burma the US serviceman could not spend a dollar – there was nothing to buy! They were very conscious of the terrible conditions under which the 14th Army lived and fought. Their airmen spared no effort to deliver their supplies. If you ever got to a US base you were treated like royalty. I remember at one base they had made a small cinema and they had used bomb crates cut in half to form small stools or seats. They insisted we move to the front of the line up. As we entered the door there were shelves full of chewing gun, chocolate, etc. We hesitantly took one and a US sergeant came up and gave us handfuls saying, "Help yourselves, fellas."

We were given tinned ice-cream etc. and a small tin with a screw cap on one end. You lit this with a match and it fizzed for a time then *voilà*, hot chocolate was ready to drink. We also were given little grenade-like bombs, which you could use in your tent. They killed every bug present and you could scoop them up in handfuls from the top of your mosquito net. This was a real luxury, no bugs while you slept.

I am sure all this attention from the Yanks was simply their recognition of the terrible conditions under which we lived and fought while in the jungle. It was never meant to show off, just to show their respect for the 14th Army. Much later I was to experience the same type of generosity when I visited Washington DC on government business.

However, life in the jungle with Indian soldiers was our most common lot. Unpolished rice was their staple diet and from a nutritional point of view, the perfect food. Fed twice per day to the British soldier it made a very boring, unappetizing diet. Fluid intake was high to prevent dehydration in the tropical heat and tea was the main source of fluid. Drinking water was scarce although there was "water, water everywhere, nor any drop to drink." This quotation from the poem, the "Ancient Mariner" took on a new and poignant meaning in the Burmese jungle.

The Burmese native population lived mainly in small villages with a village central deep well. Unfortunately, the Japanese poisoned these wells as they withdrew. Paris green containing arsenic was the usual method. The locals had to resort to small wells or springs which were relatively safe for drinking water, but often very inaccessible in the jungle clad hills. The women carried water supplies in large pots on their heads, sometimes over great distances in rough country. A gift of water from them represented a considerable amount of hard work, for which we had little to repay them. They were generally slender in stature and walked very gracefully with their heavy load on their head. I remember thinking of models in training walking with books on their heads – these ladies required no training at all.

As time passed we had contact with British units and became aware that the Japanese had suffered major defeats in the north and east of Burma. We had no idea of the scale of these battles. Indeed I was out of the army for several years before I was able to comprehend the extent of these battles. For example the battles around Kohima Imphal were among the major battles of the Second World War. Over 50,000 Japanese troops were killed at Imphal, whereas as at Alamein the total killed, wounded and missing for both sides together was somewhat less than 50,000 men. Many years later when in Ottawa I was visited by two old Japanese scientists involved in new veterinary drugs in Japan. They assured me that Imphal was the biggest defeat in the history of the Japanese army. There were numerous paperback books available in Japan on Imphal. They both shook their heads in despair when they spoke of this battle. I also discovered that West Point Military Academy in the USA gives a course on military history to their graduates and among the historic battles studied are the battle of Bannockburn in Scotland in 1314 and the battle of Imphal in 1944.

Our ignorance of the events in Burma was something I could never understand, especially when the outcome was such a boost to our morale. The net result of these Japanese defeats in the northeast of Burma was a piecemeal retreat of all Japanese forces in the north and in the west of Burma – the Arakan, towards Thailand (Siam). We did not know it then but this meant that over 50,000 Japanese troops had to find their way eastwards and cross the main Mandalay-Rangoon road and negotiate the Pegu Yomas range of mountains to reach safety in Siam where they had military bases and where they could regroup. Thus large group of Nips were emerging from jungle tracts to cross the main road south to Rangoon. These units were in bad shape and pretty desperate for supplies of any kind. The road south itself was undefended except for isolated posts usually in villages along the way. Rangoon was supposed to be taken from the sea by a separate army – invasion style.

Our orders such as they were, instructed us to make our way to an Indian engineer unit near Rangoon and Mingaladon airfield. For eight men and one officer with no transport and only rifles and a little ammunition, this was a tall order as the distance was about 300 or more miles. We had to harbour during the hours of darkness in villages or strong points as best we could. If we encountered the remnants of a Japanese division emerging from a track we were out of luck.

Before our push for Rangoon I had some misfortune. I suffered an injury to my right hand and my right ring finger had become badly infected. An open wound sustained in the jungle can become easily infected. An Indian medical officer treated me at a field ambulance but the wound became worse and purulent. I was flown out to a base hospital in the north in Burdwan Province east of Bengal. There I was quickly operated on by an Anglo-Indian surgeon. When I recovered from the anaesthetic my right arm was in a splint and it was held upright to the mosquito net. This was to assist in drainage of the wound. There was no penicillin, only M&Bs (sulphon-amide drugs). The gauze drain inserted into my wound was soon removed and the hole stitched up. I was very lucky my tendons were all OK and functional and my hand restored to near normal.

The short stay in hospital was great. I got good food as I remembered it and no rice or chapattis. My neighbour in the next bed was an infantry man who had a Japanese bullet in his shoulder. The Japanese rifle bullet is quite small, a little more than a 22 rifle bullet but it is discharged from the long Japanese rifle with very high muzzle velocity. They had

X-rayed this man several times then rushed him into the theatre to remove it. All without success. He had another X-ray and they announced they finally could now remove it, they failed again. The surgeon then told him it was below his scapula (shoulder blade) and as it went in pretty hot, was probably sterile and they were going to leave it there as it presented no hazard. He was greatly relieved.

We had only three records for a wind up gramophone in this hospital ward. They were played over and over again every day. Every time I hear the Ink Spots or Deanna Durbin singing the "Lights of Home", I am transported in thought back to that hospital.

I remember Sister MacIntosh, the army nursing sister in charge of the ward. Like many of her kind, she was worth her weight in gold and was definitely in charge of the ward. We had a small Hindu sweeper boy who crouched down on his heels as he swept the floor with a long switch. This is still common today in India especially in the poorer districts – no vacuum cleaners! This boy just worshipped Sister MacIntosh. Unfortunately, he took malaria and Sister MacIntosh put him in a spare bed at the end of the ward. No one dared object! When the Anglo-Indian surgeon did his rounds she asked him to take a look at this boy. He produced a silk handkerchief from his breast pocket and laid it over the boy's wrist to take his pulse. Sister MacIntosh was not amused, and brusquely removed the silk handkerchief and snapped, "I will take his pulse, doctor." It was an incredible scene. This well qualified and educated Anglo-Indian surgeon would not want to touch a poor sweeper. It was a demonstration of just how deep the class system ruled India.

I have since discussed this incident with well-educated

Indians in Canada, some forty years later, and they did not seem perturbed by this discrimination. I suppose in our own culture similar discrimination was once common in the UK many years ago. When I arrived in India, our troops regarded the Indian soldiers as "Wogs" and not very civilized or sophisticated. However, close contact with Indian soldiers on active service soon dispelled such attitudes. Generally, I found them very reliable, kind and helpful when they were treated with respect. My only exception was a Sikh unit we camped beside on one occasion. We asked them where we could bivouac for the night and they directed us just before dark to a sandy spot beside a river. We took their word in good faith, but during the night discovered we were sleeping close to a mound of sand by the edge of the river. The Sikhs apparently had killed some Japanese and piled them in a heap and threw some sand over them. The place stank. The Sikhs were an arrogant bunch.

I did serve with other units which contained some Sikhs and never encountered any difficulties. It is worth mentioning that the Indian National Army recruited by the Japanese contained a very high proportion of Sikhs, about 100,000, mainly deserters from the Indian Army. They were called jiffs. I remember a plane load of them, nearly all big six-foot Sikhs, were unloading through the gap in the fuselage of a Dakota transport plane at an airfield. Two small five foot tall Gurkhas were standing at each side of the door of the plane. They were kicking the Sikhs out of the plane with utter contempt on their faces. Of course if these traitors made one wrong move, out would have come the *kukri* and a Sikh would have lost more than just his hair. The loyalty of these little soldiers was never in question and their utter contempt for these traitors was indescribable. I remember hearing after the war, Montgomery had complaints about the 5th Indian Division in the desert, from the German Afrika Korps. I believe the Sikh units were involved.

Back among my mates, life was much the same and I was glad to be back with the men I had come to know so well. Our tasks were fairly routine – mostly dealing with unexploded shells or mortar bombs. I often thought the Japanese had a fairly high failure rate with their explosives. Perhaps it was their exposure to the continual damp conditions which affected them. The Nips used to fire their shells or mortar bombs in fours. Sometimes you would hear boom, boom, boom, thud. We would then say, "Oh, another for us." This means we would have to explode it if it lay in a dangerous spot, e.g. on a track. Anything which landed in remote bush was generally difficult to find and if of little consequence was left untouched.

In 1945 as the Japs became more desperate they resorted to some repulsive tactics. Our Indian unit overran a Japanese field ambulance and found a row of Japanese dead, all lying in a nice straight line, but all shot in the side of the head. Obviously done by their own men rather than leave them to be captured. Apparently our medics thought we could have saved some of them.

The Nips had also taken to setting booby-traps on their own and our dead. Generally a grenade or charge was placed under them so that when we moved them for burial we sustained casualties – sometimes fatal. Consequently, we never tried to neutralize these charges, we merely attached some signal cable around the ankles and at a safe distance gave it a quick heave. We never encountered a booby-trap here, but these precautions were unfortunately very necessary to save our own lives. We had learned this from the experience of other units. It was a despicable act and apart from humanity, and something which would never have been done by a British unit. We were never really surprised by anything the Nips did, although they fought very bravely, often to the last man.

Our work with explosives was almost routine, but to the infantryman we were held in high esteem. It was ironical when we encountered men returning from a long patrol in the jungle and soaked and exhausted, they would often say "I would not have your job for a pension." On balance, I always thought we had the much better lot.

Almost always we were deprived of up-to-date news about the course of the Burma campaign and often we were unsure of exactly where we were. However, at long last we knew the Japanese were on the run and we were ordered south to near Rangoon and Mingladon airfield. We knew Rangoon had been taken from the sea and that things were moving fast now and in our favour. We were ill prepared for such a journey. We had some army fourteen-man ration packs, a little drinking water and ammunition – but no transport at all. We travelled very light. We reached Tongoo, a small town in the middle of Burma with an airstrip nearby. We merely skirted the town and marched southward. We did not know it then but Tongoo had been fiercely contested by the retreating Japanese.

As we trudged southwards we had a tremendous bit of luck. Along came a convoy of five military ambulances headed for Pegu which was a strategic town about 200 miles south and where there had been some savage battles. The convoy had only five Indian drivers and one British medical officer. Naturally he was delighted to have us as passengers and at least some support if attacked. We eagerly climbed aboard and set off under the Red Cross, armed of course. Not that this means anything in this campaign. The Japanese would attack anything that moved, Red Cross and all. I got into the last ambulance with my burly mate. It was so comfortable we could have lain down and slept. However, we were warned to be alert with one up the spout at all times. In case of ambush we were to get into the nearest monsoon ditch by the roadside and defend our trucks.

We saw almost nothing for hours, except new roadside graves of Indians, British and Japanese. What we did not know was that large desperate Jap units were emerging from the jungle tracks and heading eastward toward Siam. They were in terrible shape and short of everything. It was pure luck that we managed to miss them for I later learned that some 50,000 Japs were involved in this retreat across the main Tongoo-Rangoon road.

We had some lighter moments. My burly mate saw a duck in a large pond alongside the road and with a view to having roast duck, he shot it. The convoy came to an abrupt halt and the MO came hurrying to the rear ambulance. He immediately looked at me and gave me hell. After he was finished berating me about the dangers of ambush, my mate confessed his sin. He escaped censure at my expense. Probably, as I was much younger, he thought I was the obvious culprit. Ironically a 303 bullet hitting a duck leaves little worth roasting. We had a good laugh later on.

By nightfall we had reached the village or Nyanglabin and were ordered to harbour for the night. The road marshal was an Australian officer and was quite a character. He directed us to the schoolhouse by the roadside where we could sleep out of the constant monsoon rain. The building was like many native huts and sat on large teak pillars which kept it dry. We slept on the floor and it was quite comfortable for a change. Our main concern was fresh water. We scrounged water from the local garrison of Indian soldiers.

By daybreak we were on our way as the five ambulances were urgently needed at Pegu. This was not a comforting thought as we had to go well beyond Pegu to reach the Indian engineering unit we were supposed to join. On our way south we picked up a young RAF pilot who had come down by parachute close to the main road. He was really relieved to join us. We would help him reach the RAF at Mingaladon airfield near Rangoon.

We passed almost no traffic going north and saw nothing going south. We did see one 15-cwt truck with a real live Japanese under escort inside. This was unusual as they seldom surrendered or were taken alive. It was a good sign that even the Nips were getting desperate as their situation was hopeless. Eventually we approached Pegu but were halted north of the town. We were told to wait as only artillery was being allowed over the bridge. We wandered down to a large river probably the Sittang and soon found the gunners with their 25-pounders busy shelling the enemy. I remember helping to bring up the shells to the guns as we had little else to do but wait. The gunners were glad of the help as they were working hard on half rations. I did not mind as it was not often we had a chance to hit back at the Nips, as we were usually on the receiving end of their 75s or mortars.

I learned later that thousands of Japs had been killed trying to escape over to the other side of this huge river. The bodies were floating downstream for days afterwards. At last, because the ambulances were badly needed, we were allowed to cross and were soon outside Pegu. As we approached we were faced by a row of Bofors anti-aircraft guns with their gun barrels depressed horizontally. Apparently the Nips tried to recover Pegu the day before and the gunners used the Bofors with great effect on them. We wasted no time in Pegu – only long enough to scrounge some water and food. Unfortunately, we had to leave our ambulances and start to march southwards again.

Luck was with us as once more a 3-ton truck picked us up and we headed for our new unit. Several miles north of Rangoon we found our Royal Engineers unit. The CO was a major and had a Scottish accent. He immediately recognized my superior English. He asked where I was from then laughed at my reply. He lived about four miles from my home and owned a large brickworks in a neighbouring small town in Scotland. He had little to give us but he did his best to provide a fairly decent place to live and a tent for our mess room.

Our new billet was a tall Burmese building with an intact roof but no walls – only wooden pillars from which all the siding had been stripped and stolen. With typical Royal Engineer's ingenuity we wrapped canvas hessian around the pillars and made a fully respectable house. We made a platform on each side to sleep on which was off the ground and we made a rough toilet with three holes over a trench. We wrapped canvas around it and made a fairly respectable toilet. Unfortunately, the Indian engineers had no European food for us so we had to make the best of it.

The Indian unit had a large engineers' stores dump with all kinds of tools and building equipment which was beginning to arrive from the port of Rangoon. Only two jetties were operational due to bombing and demolition by us and by the

Japanese. As cargo was unloaded in a great hurry then transported by trucks to various units, it was rather a mix up. All army stores are marked by their own particular sign for engineers or ordinance etc. The haste to unload was such that often a lot of Ordinance Corps stores would arrive among engineers stores. This chaos had some advantages, e.g. bales of olive-green army jersey pullovers landed in our depot. Also olive-green army towels, gumboots etc.

There were numerous native coolies who came to work as labour at our depot. They were mostly small, thin Tamils from south India but they had chickens and eggs and even some flour. Naturally we bartered our spare pullovers and boots etc. for much needed food. It was strange and comical to see these little Tamils and even their kids going around with rolled up oversized pullovers and rubber boots with a big smile on their round black faces. On the other hand, we had fried eggs (very small ones as everything was small and stunted) and of course chickens without rice. It was great to have normal food again.

We did have a scare over the rubber boots as we got to know that some Ordinance Corps officer was searching for them. We put the few that remained down the toilet trench and added some lime. When he poked his nose down the hole he was greeted by a cloud of stinking steam from the lime. He soon left in a hurry.

Life here was restful after our hectic time up north. We used the equipment carried by this Indian unit to make beds, tables, kit boxes etc. We had two experienced carpenters in our group and they were delighted with the equipment and trained the Indians in its use.

I had a great stroke of luck at this unit. One day an RAF officer came in and asked for some iron pickets to erect a

Dannet wire fence. There were still stray Japanese around Mingaladon airfield and he was setting up defence around his aircraft. I asked him if he had any news of 31 Squadron RAF, as my brother was on Ramree island with them off the coast of Burma. He said some 31 Squadron had just arrived at Mingaladon and he took my brother's name and number. To my surprise my brother arrived the very next afternoon at our camp. The officer had kept his word. My brother John was an iron moulder in civvy street, but a cook in the RAF. This was typical of the forces. In India our head cook was a concreter grade D2 in the Royal Engineers. We discovered the connection in the mess hall!

Of course the Navy and the Air Force seemed to lack for nothing in the way of rations. My brother was shocked at our meals – mainly rice and what we could get by bartering goods. He thought we were starving. I guess none of us were in good physical shape. The very next day John returned to our unit with loads of food *à la* RAF. Loaves of fresh bread, eggs, bacon, tins of all sorts. I was very popular. The most frequent question was, "When is your brother coming back?"

Our billet was fairly comfortable, but at night we were bothered by packs of piards or wild dogs. These were big, lean, rough dogs, like heavy greyhounds, which came barking and fighting around our camp at night. We decided to fix them and laid in wait for them one night with our rifles loaded. We fired a volley and killed a few of them. One bullet hit the spinous process on the scapula of a dog and went backwards and severed its ribs on one side. We discovered later that there were some shallow Japanese graves around with a little Japanese shovel stuck upside down in the ground to mark them. The dogs were after the bodies for food, a horrible thought!

Life was relatively peaceful in our new unit. Our mail was sometimes two months old by the time it reached us. My twentieth birthday had come and gone a long time before I got my mail. When the mail did arrive my burly mate dumped a carton box covered in tattered brown paper on the ground. Immediately swarms of ants streamed out from it over the ground. My poor old mother had managed to obtain all the scarce ingredients for a birthday cake. Unfortunately she had no idea about the insect life in the East. My cake was quickly transferred to the toilet trench. Ah well, "the best laid schemes o' mice and men, gang aft a-gley and lea'e us nought but grief and pain for promised joy" – apologies to Robbie Burns.

Life was fairly tranquil until one day in August 1945 when an RAF officer came in to collect some stores. He told us a new type of bomb had been dropped on Japan and the war would soon be over. We laughed and joked the same as we did with all rumours. However, about five days later we heard a great deal of shouting coming from the direction of Rangoon. We immediately thought the Nips had launched a counter offensive to retake Rangoon. We were busily preparing to defend this depot when someone arrived and told us the war was over. They had dropped another new bomb on Japan and they had surrendered unconditionally. We had difficulty believing this, knowing the Japs' tenacity.

We had no transport – only a dumper truck with a big scoop in front for carrying earth. We all climbed into it and drove to Rangoon with our rifles. The place was like a madhouse. Troops were shooting into the night air and everyone was going crazy. Yes, the war was really over and of course the first thought of my older comrades was for their

speedy return home. I knew I would have little chance of that
at my age.

News of the Japanese surrender transformed our everyday
conversation. The Army had been ordered by the Cabinet to
return all men who had served in the Far East for more than
three years and four months, as soon as possible. This had not
been received well by the top brass as they wanted experienced
troops for the invasion of Malaya and recapture of Singapore.
Replacements from the UK which would be largely, young
inexperienced men did not appeal to the general staff. The
end of the war did however transform all these plans and
projections. It was more than ever important to return these
veterans. Some of them had not seen their wives and children
for four years or more.

General Slim had ordered his Chief Medical Officer, a Dr.
Young, to assess the medical fitness of his fighting units before
embarking on the recapture of Malaya. The results were shock-
ing to the top brass but not to the fighting units. The British
soldiers were, in general, suffering from malnutrition and
exhaustion. Of course this was not made public until after the
war but we knew the score without any survey by looking at
our thin tired bodies. Our hopes of better rations and some
rest never materialized. In fact, sometimes I thought we
received poorer rations than during the war.

Now all talk centred on repatriation to the UK. For this
purpose the army gave you a group number for release from
the services. These groups were based on age and the amount
of service in the army. They ranged from 1 to 70 or 80 or
more. My small detachment were "old" men except for two
of us. My mate was 28 and I had just turned 20. The rest
were all in their thirties and forties. Their group ranged from

groups of 8 to 10, 11, 12. My mate I believe was group 30. My group was 60. They all chalked their group numbers on the end of their beds. Of course, mine was a cruel joke! They used to joke that peacetime service in India was a minimum of seven years, but I was just a kid anyway with no wife or children. They were not to know that before long I would be recalled to my old unit which would consist of young recruits and I would be the only man with active service in Burma. I would become the "old soldier" or "old sweat" which was the expression given to an experienced soldier out in the Far East.

The repatriation of men from Burma was not without incident since it was a very sensitive subject and held precedence over any other issue. Apparently in the transit camp in Rangoon a group of war weary men were promised embarkation on the next ship for the UK. At the last moment this group was replaced by Indian units destined to reoccupy Singapore and take charge of thousands of Japanese prisoners of war. When this became known, all hell broke loose in the camp. There was a riot and an ugly situation. In typical army fashion a high ranking officer – I believe a general – arrived to quell the riot. In a condescending manner he tried to brow beat these disgusted men but was quickly shouted down and his aide-de-camp who was spotted taking notes was roughly ejected.

The situation in the camp was very volatile as the projected move of the Indians to Singapore went ahead. However the very next day Lord Mountbatten arrived by air and went straight to address the waiting men at the transit camp. There was absolutely no formality. He climbed onto a table and asked the men to gather round him. This was his style as I had

previously encountered at an airfield in Burma. He apologised
to the men and named a ship and its date of arrival in Rangoon.
He merely said, "You will all be on it for England." A great
cheer went up and he abruptly left the scene. This situation
was soon restored to normal. The men knew this time it was
for real. Maybe at last the top brass were beginning to realize
that there was a definite swing in the attitude of our weary
men. They were prepared to serve loyally during the war, but
peacetime was a whole new ball game. The ruling class was
in for a big shock at the forthcoming election.

In my little world there was little change. We worked very
hard to distribute all the necessary engineering supplies for
reconstruction and repair of war damage. We had a flock of
coolie labour from a nearby settlement of Tamils from South
India. I had about a dozen small boys ranging up to age 12
to deal with small stores such as tools, nails etc. They came
seven days per week from their village across the other side
of a lake. They walked miles to work carrying a little sack of
rice to sustain themselves. They were happy children and
worked well for half a rupee a day – about nine pence or
twenty cents.

I used to teach them English and they learned to count in
English very quickly. They were intelligent kids. I would
collect all the emergency ration chocolate bars, line up the
boys at the end of work and distribute this awful stuff as fairly
as possible. It was highly nutritious but tasted blah! It always
brought a big toothsome grin to their little round black faces.
They would volunteer to do washing or clean kit or boots.
For this they wanted only a cigarette. Much to my shame I
did pay them this way as it was their earnest wish. It was
amusing to see a little round black happy face with a big Players

cigarette hanging from the mouth. *C'est la vie!* When it came time for me to leave, one smart little boy asked me to take him with him as my servant. I had great difficulty explaining why that could not be possible and he had great difficulty in understanding his rejection.

Our new found peace was not without incident. There were many Japanese stragglers in the area who had been isolated and knew nothing of the Japanese surrender. Invariably they avoided contact but if cornered fought and died without knowledge of their country's defeat. In addition, Burma has long been plagued by bands of robbers called dacoits who plundered to sustain themselves. To this day they infest Burma and are a source of trouble.

One evening we were startled by rifle fire from the Tamil village over the lake. There was a lot of shouting and screaming. We were in no doubt that the villagers were being attacked by dacoits. Being an engineering unit we had folding boat equipment which we quickly assembled and launched to paddle over to the village. We went well armed for battle. We drove the dacoits off into the jungle and saved the village – our source of labour. Not much was stolen, only a little rice from the poor villagers. The dacoits fled into the jungle whence they had come. We may have hit a few but we were not about to pursue them into the jungle. I was sure they would not return. The villagers were happy to be rescued as the dacoits would have cleaned them out and probably killed a few as well. Every society has its parasites and they don't all use force of arms to get what they want.

At last the big day came for me. My parent unit in Assam had been sent to Singapore to reoccupy it from the Japanese. I was to be recalled with another sergeant who had been recently sent to us as a replacement. The others, all my old mates would soon be repatriated back to UK for demobilization. It was, in a way, a sad day and farewell, alas, for ever.

We boarded a small troop ship which had been built at Barkley Curles Shipyard in Glasgow. A shipyard where I had worked one summer as an apprentice naval architect. We joined an Indian field regiment for the journey from Rangoon to Singapore. I slept on the open deck among the Indians. The nights were warm and still as our convoy sailed down the Malaca Straights. One evening there was a huge bang and a vivid flash up ahead. We were stationary for hours afterwards. Apparently a freighter up ahead had hit a stray Japanese mine and her bow was damaged but not too seriously. I hoped there were no more stray mines up ahead.

As usual the Indian cooks had their galley up on deck and they shared their hospitality with us. One evening we sat around in a small circle singing and chatting. In the middle was a large bucket full of pineapple rings. The cooks had withheld these from the daily rations for a party. Some Rosa rum appeared from nowhere and the party was on. No knives, forks or spoons or glasses. We fished out the pineapple rings with our fingers and one olive-green mug served as a glass. Despite my limited Urdu and their lack of English, we managed to communicate and enjoyed their comradeship. It was a strange yet satisfying experience: and there was mutual respect. This was the kind of alliance which had defeated the mighty Japanese armies.

Soon we were in Singapore – a bustling city which had suffered some war damage, particularly around the harbour. Huge chunks of wrecked ships lay against the sea wall, although the harbour was relatively clear. We were soon disembarked and whisked away to our old parent unit outside the city. It was rather strange for me as many of the older men had been left in India for repatriation and there were numerous new faces, mostly recently arrived from the UK. Naturally it was not the same as my old unit, but I had to get used to it.

My old Colonel was still in charge and he sent for me the next day. He was still very patronizing and obviously still disliked me. The feeling was mutual. I had outlived the bastard!

We were billeted in a large oriental, two-storey building with doors every six feet and verandas all around. Sheer luxury with charpois beds – wooden frames with string mattresses. Our food of course was terrible. Poor quality and scarce. My first breakfast was porridge, English style, with sugar in it not salt, plus one tiny piece of hard fried bacon and a small slice of fried bread. Lunch and dinner were no better. At least here I could go into Singapore and buy a square meal in the many cafes now in business. Our CO addressed us one day and told us the reason for our poor diet was that we were broke! This, of course, did not extend to the Officers' Mess and we had numerous officers of all ranks. God alone knows why! They never seemed to do any useful work.

My first day at work in a huge stores depot was in No 2 yard at Shed 2A – a large corrugated iron building the size of a large house, with a few Nissen huts around it. This was destined to store all the building tools from hammers to theodolites and all manner of nails, bolts and house fittings.

When I arrived there I was shocked to see almost a thousand Japanese prisoners. Little stalky sunburnt ugly bundles of cheap cotton. I was filled with hate and contempt for these savage little "Sons of Heaven" from Nippon.

This hatred was well founded. Fighting soldiers in general

have a high respect for their enemy as soldiers, be they victors or vanquished. In this case the feeling was quite the reverse. It was one of contempt and vengeance. I should explain the reason for this state of mind.

While near Mingaladon airfield north of Rangoon when the war ended our little detachment had much less work to do. We volunteered to help bring back Allied prisoners of war with the RAF. Needless to say we flew in armed and the RAF were glad of our help. On arrival at Bangkok airfield there was no sign of any Japanese. A few Siamese pointed us in the direction of a rough bamboo hangar nearby. We ran over to see if any POWs were there. We were absolutely shocked at the scene inside. There were many POWs, some on rough bamboo stretchers with rough amputations of legs and arms. Poor emaciated living skeletons usually covered in tropical ulcers of their bare legs and bodies. They were gaunt and spaced out. They had a vile stench from the tropical ulcers due to Leishmaniasis. My big burly mate was overwhelmed by the smell. Tough as he was he made for the door and went outside and vomited repeatedly. He was so overwhelmed we could not assist them. My feeling was one of outrage how anyone could treat these POWs in this manner. If any Nips had turned up I would have gladly shot them on the spot.

These poor souls were quite overwhelmed to see us. We did what we could to encourage them and cheer them up. We had gone around the RAF and scrounged some beer, cigarettes and chocolate for the POWs.

We carried them into the Dakota and wrapped them up in jungle blankets which luckily we had brought with us. There were no seats in the cargo Dakota aircraft but we set them down on the floor which was sloping towards the tail with their heads towards the cabin. We explained that we must fly over the Pegu Yomas range of mountains to reach Rangoon and as we had no oxygen they must lie quietly during this part of the flight. These poor men knew nothing of the progress of the war except that the Germans had surrendered earlier.

On reflection I always thought these poor men behaved with remarkable composure at such a moment after their long ordeal. We soon transferred them to army ambulances at Mingaladon airfield – perhaps even the same ones which had taken us south from Tongoo to Pegu.

We conveyed them to the University of Rangoon which was fairly unscathed after the bombing and shelling. The Army had turned the university into a hospital. For weeks no one could see a doctor or a dentist. They were all very busy with these poor POWs. No one ever complained. I inquired from a medical officer who informed me that these men were being given treatment then flown to Darjeeling, a hill station and rest camp in the Himalayas in the north of India. There they would be dewormed, and well fed before going by hospital ship to the UK and demob.

This disgusting experience I put in the back of my memory but it was never to be erased. Consequently, the first sight of these well fed Japanese POWs in Singapore filled me with hate and retribution. Their arrogant officers made me particularly vengeful. They would be carefully scrutinized by me at all times. I remember seeing the film *Bridge on the River Kwai*, it was mild and sedate compared to the real thing.

The Japanese blamed or excused their barbarity towards helpless prisoners on their military code. One Japanese officer once told me it was ungentlemanly to surrender. I asked him why he had surrendered and he quickly told me, capitulation was different. I told him it was merely surrender *en masse* and, therefore, according to his code, he should kill himself and I would give him every facility to do so. His face twisted in anger and I was ready to respond if he made one wrong move. He quickly took his departure. I had made him lose face and I was well satisfied with that. From then onwards I was to employ this practice whenever I was faced with Japanese arrogance. Strangely enough I must have become the most respected soldier in my unit.

All the troops in my unit had come from India or straight out from the UK. They had little knowledge of Burma or the Japanese. I was put in charge of Shed 2A in our depot and I was given a young Chinese man (Michael Phang) to assist me. He spoke English well and also some Japanese and of course Cantonese. He had been a teacher but was recruited by the Japanese into a shipping company. Unknown to him this was a Japanese spy ring during the war. I also had two Jewish men, evacuated from Batavia, Ezekel and his son-in-law Izzi. They spoke English and Dutch and some Japanese and made good clerks and storekeepers. I also had two Japanese POWs every day to assist me. One had been a trainee pilot – Nangahashi and he spoke no English. The other was an engineer attached to the army. This was common in their army. His name was Komota and he spoke good English. He was not a military type at all and I think hated the army – even as an attached civilian.

It was a motley crew – a Scot, a Chinese, two Japanese, Jews and Nips. To this we had as required about twenty Malaya and Chinese coolie women and at times a few Japanese POWs to do heavy manual labour. As soon as my old Colonel had left for England I was promoted quite quickly to lance-corporal and then corporal then lance-sergeant then sergeant and finally staff sergeant. My final rank was very useful when handling the Japanese.

One Japanese explained to me, "Japanese army, No. 1 – lieutenant i.e. the lieutenant was the most important man. British Army No.1, sergeant master. I should explain that Japanese POWs of all ranks were made to address all our men as Master. I insisted on this from all Japanese officers. The sergeants on active service wore their stripes on their epaulets, not on their sleeves. This was so they could be removed easily. It was no secret that the Japanese would select a sergeant if they could. When I recall my whole army career, the sergeants were the men who got everything done. My brother-in-law, who became a medical officer in the army in Italy, told me if he had any bother with malingerers he merely threatened them with the sergeant and the problem was quickly solved.

Most of the time the work was tedious but occasionally we had a few laughs. There was one very arrogant Japanese, Lieutenant Nagata. He had been a pilot and spoke excellent English. He was as arrogant as they come. My ploy with him was to belittle him as much as possible, especially in front of the Chinese. One day I had the Japanese carrying coils of barb wire between them on a pole. They weighted them on a spring balance and Lieutenant Nagata had the job of adding up the weights on a blackboard with white chalk. I spotted a little error in his arithmetic. When my group were close by I drew his attention to his mistake. I said, "When will you teach Scottish mathematics in Japan, where $1 + 1 = 2$ and not 3." I had him real well.

Not to be outdone he arrived one day with a page from a geometry book with a deduction for me to solve. I soon caught on to his scheme. I surveyed it quickly then handed it back to him. He urged me to solve it, but I said "O.K. leave it there until I can get some free time. My Colonel wants this job finished soon and I must supervise it now. I will look at it for you later if I find some time." He seemed satisfied. Of course I knew it would be fairly difficult and I sent him to supervise his men some distance away. I soon worked out the answer after some deep thinking and determination to humble Nagata.

Later that afternoon Nagata arrived with another Nip officer, obviously to gloat over his deduction. I said OK give me some time to study it and come back in ten or fifteen minutes. All bows and smiles they left. Of course, I had already figured it out and had not even looked at it since they left. I grudgingly went and picked it up and puzzled over it for a few minutes. I then said Ah! I handed them the solution much to their dismay. As I left I made a late polite bow and they immediately bowed real low. Of course my staff were grinning all over which upset the arrogant Nips more than anything. They had lost face again. I told them I really had no time for such elementary academic exercises. I had work to do and so had they. Hyaku! (hurry up)

Nagata was still determined to try to be superior. One day he was to supervise the cleaning of all our officers' revolvers. Our CO had an old World War I weapon and Nagata inquired sarcastically why British officers used such old fashioned weapons.

I retorted, "Why do Japanese officers carry old swords?"

He immediately replied, "To cut British soldiers' heads off."

I calmly said, "Oh really," and as I turned away the iron heel plate of my army boot came down with a turning pressure on his bare toes as he wore simple chaplis or wooden soles with a wide strap over the instep. He groaned in pain and I immediately apologized for the accident. All this in front of the Chinese. I think Nagata learned not to provoke me in any way. Strangely enough, my standing with the Japanese prisoners seemed to be raised.

My own two regulars were eager to please. I talked more and more to Komota who was an engineer in civil life and understood English well. We talked of home and university and financing education. We had a lot in common in this respect and we even discussed our life after demob. I realized that deep down under all the military facade we were not altogether different. We had the same aspirations and hopes. He was an imperial slave of the Japanese army and I was a war-weary volunteer who had done his duty just like him and longed for a peaceful life. He even encouraged me not to worry and to try hard to get back to university. I was beginning to realize that he was controlled by military tradition and obedience; and I was an army volunteer fighting to preserve a system of privilege for a selected group of well-heeled upper middle class. I had serious doubts that this system would ever change.

Singapore had an agreeable climate. Fairly hot but the Trade Winds blew over the island and there was usually some convectional rainfall in short showers every few days. We did have a wet season but nothing like the monsoon in Burma. I normally worked wearing only shorts as I had the type of skin which browns easily and deeply. I quickly resembled an oriental gentleman with a round black face. The Japanese POWs were also quite brown. One lunch break I saw my Colonel coming, and not wishing to be pestered by his endless prattle I sat down among a ring of Nips with my hat off and one of their mess tins in front of me. The CO walked straight past much to the amusement of the Japanese. The Japanese had a somewhat childish sense of humour.

In our unit there was always a joker who must not be allowed free reign. One day the Nips were carrying bags of cement on their backs to a railway car. The work was being hindered by the resident joker. As he passed by the cement stack I lifted another bag of cement and placed it on top of his load. His knees buckled and he swore, then the large bags broke on the ground around him. He was like an off-white snow man. All hell broke loose and the Nips were laughing loudly, some writhing in paroxysms on the floor. I made the joker clean it up of course and thereafter the work went very smoothly. I had learned a lesson.

On another occasion we were loading timber onto railway trucks. We had acquired a new captain who fancied himself as a slave driver and also prided himself for his knowledge of Japanese. He berated the Nips swinging a pick handle and yelling "Quekay" (pronounced as shown). The Nips all bowed and smiled then took a break. The more he yelled the more they relaxed. He saw that I was amused and reprimanded me saying, I expect you could get this loaded faster.

I said, "if you wish, sir."

He challenged me to do it.

I put on my bush hat which made me look like an Aussie for whom the Nips had high respect. I yelled, "Keoatski" which means attention, and the Nips all stood to attention. I then yelled, "Hiaku" which means hurry up and they all worked like beavers to finish the job. I said, "Quekay" (break time) and "Yoroshi" (very good).

The brave captain stood in amazement and said, "I said

that." I never did tell him his only comment meant "break time". We won the war despite these types.

The Nips organized a sports day at this camp and I was approached by Lieutenant Nagata to compete. I declined as I knew they were training hard for it and he hoped to humble me. I apologized but said I had no time but I would challenge him to a 100-yard race right now. He declined and lost face again.

My regular Japanese helper Nangahashi had a habit of arriving on his own very early every morning. When I arrived at 8.00 am there would be a dish with beautiful flowers in it on my desk. He replaced these regularly as he knew I liked to grow flowers. I asked the Japanese interpreter to ask him where he obtained the flowers. He just smiled. He obviously was raiding the local gardens very early in the morning. I explained I could not protect him if he was caught. He just smiled and the flowers kept coming. He was a highly intelligent Nip and very clean. He had only one shirt. I had a spare olive-green bush shirt which I gave to him. He found an old sewing machine which he made to function and he remodelled the shirt to fit him quite neatly. He wore it one day and his Japanese one the next, always clean.

The Nips of course were sent home before we were. On his last day I bade him farewell and he was in tears. I learned from the interpreter that his home had been in Hiroshima and he had no idea about the fate of his relatives.

We had several Chinese and Eurasian girls working as clerks and typists. One very attractive lady worked our telephone exchange. She was very aloof and obviously disliked the English. Even our new colonel, straight out from the War Office, received short shrift from her.

At Christmas the troops generally embark on a 24-hour drunken binge. I was asked to operate the telephone exchange as I was not a drinker and being a Scot I celebrated New Year's Day. I agreed, but I required instruction from "Elizabeth the beautiful". She was rather sharp at first. When I asked her to repeat something she said "Oh, you English." I, of course, reprimanded her, saying that I was not English, I was Scottish. Are you Japanese, I asked, and she changed her attitude completely.

I learned the Japanese had taken away her husband to the Siam Railway where he perished. The British military administration had done little to meet her claim for compensation and she was naturally quite bitter. She had been a dentist's receptionist before the war and those homely white women obviously resented their husbands' ogling her. Poor lady, she was neither English nor Chinese but had obviously acquired the best of both races. She was indeed beautiful and very elegant but obviously suffered from a complex. I did my best to assure her that the white women were very jealous of her and very protective of their husbands. As for myself, I was Scottish and never English and not to insult me.

She was always very friendly to me especially when she was getting on the truck with the other Chinese girls to be taken back to the city after work. I got a lot of ribbing from my mates over this but I kept my secret.

We obtained a large collection of new officers – all hearty types just out from Sandhurst. Their Mess was apparently a mess in reality. Now our Sergeants' and Warrant Officers' Mess was like a palace.

The Japanese POWs all carried a card with their identification and their civilian occupation. We had all the building material and I arranged with my sergeant major – an old regular soldier – to have a dance floor with a small bandstand installed. I arranged for a Japanese artist to paint picture on all the panels between the oriental doors all around the room. I supplied the paint and the artist brushes he made from ordinary paint brushes. I also had polishing dumpers like those used in hospitals to polish the floors. Two men polishing for five minutes then ten minutes rest, a squad of six Nips in all. The floor was just like a professional ballroom.

The artist painted large murals on the walls of our dining room. They were taken from magazines showing plates of delicious food. We also hung an old soccer ball from the roof. We had spicules of coloured glass in the ball just like a giant chestnut. As the fans turned so did the ball throwing beams of coloured light in all directions. We hired a local Hawaiian guitar band for a dance in our mess. The guys christened the band the Hawaiian Jockstraps.

The trouble with holding dances was that there were over 3,000 troops in Singapore and only about thirty women, ATS and a few nurses plus a few Civil Service women of doubtful value. Posters for dances etc. were pinned on the ATS guardroom but rival units would often remove them in favour of their own. I screwed ours to the wall with large wood screws. All was set and our sergeant cook who had been a London chef worked all night to prepare a terrific buffet for the dance.

I casually mentioned in the mess that I would like to invite Elizabeth, our telephone operator. I received the usual derision from my mates as to my success. I did approach Elizabeth and, of course, she was very apprehensive. She said there would be white women there and she feared being snubbed. I assured her that she would be with me and the boys would be too busy looking at her to bother with the other women. I sounded out the men in our mess about Elizabeth coming to our dance and I immediately was offered bets that I could not deliver her. My sergeant major even offered his jeep and driver if I could bring her. I discussed this with Elizabeth and stressed how the boys all would like her to attend. She was still very unsure. I told her about all the bets offered and all she had to do was come for a short time plus the buffet and a jeep was available to take her to and from her home. I then suggested with all the money from the bets we could have a nice dinner at the famous Raffles hotel. She finally agreed.

As I escorted her into our mess there was a groan from all those who laid bets. My sergeant major was the most gracious and invited us to his table. No one dared say anything to him. Our colonel arrived and almost fell on his butt when he crossed over the polished dance floor. I heard there was a great deal of grumbling about their Officers' Mess after seeing our efforts. The Colonel challenged them to do the same but they had neither the expertise nor imagination to do the job.

Elizabeth behaved in her usual gracious but aloof style. We had a great dinner at the Raffles hotel on the bet winnings. We had an ardent Casanova warrant officer who later tried his luck with Elizabeth. She gave him a real brush off as soon as she heard his English accent. I kept my secret and was amused at comments directed at my association with Elizabeth but I always treated her with great respect and kindness.

The Eurasian community was quite a small group in Singapore and of course they were neither Chinese nor English which meant they were isolated socially. It was not difficult to see why the white women on the island did not want them around.

Although the war was over and we were wearily awaiting our demobilization, life was not always dull in Singapore. The Japanese had done little to control venereal disease and after their surrender many prostitutes descended on the city as there were thousands of troops there. Venereal disease escalated and "Out of Bounds" signs which were red circles with a black multiplication cross appeared everywhere. The troops called these bicycle wheels and paid them little attention. When the Whites started to drift back from the UK to take up their old way of life they protested loudly about these signs. The Army in its wisdom decided to remove the signs and made whole districts of the city "Out of Bounds". They had army red-cap police patrols to prevent access to these districts. This had no effect on the troops as they merely considered it a challenge.

The top brass decided they would open up a club for other ranks – The Union Jack Club. It was not worth a visit. They had the bright idea of having a slogan competition for VD to deter the troops. The slogans which won it were displayed across the street at the entrance to the Out of Bounds area. They read, "Five minutes Whoopee – result VD" and "If she is game she's got it, if she's got it you have had it."

Some enterprising troops thought they would make liquor which was in short supply. Unfortunately, they used some high octane from a fuel dump and several men went blind drinking this hooch which produced another poster – "NAAFI beer is good, local booze is poison." X number of men went blind after drinking it.

The most effective deterrent to VD was an exhibition called the Green Cross. Men happily went in one door to see it and came out another rather shaken at the exit. All stages of advanced syphilis were shown including its effects on the genital organs. It was very effective and sick parades were well attended for a time thereafter.

We had our own little fiasco in our unit. We worked in a large stores dump about one-quarter of a mile long, surrounded by high barbed wire fences with towers at intervals with Bren guns on the top. We had Seaforth Highlanders or paratrooper guards manning the perimeter. We had our own generator which worked all night to illuminate the depot. The local hoods managed to contact the generator operator and paid him to let the generator fail at a certain time during the night. He agreed but told our colonel. A big trap was arranged for those thieves and some of us were selected to take CID men to hide at likely spots in the depot. I was roped in for my area which was a prime target. All went well and we were stationed before dark in our positions.

At 2 am our brave colonel drove into the depot with a company of riflemen in trucks with lights blazing. Of course the thieves were watching from the nearby trees and knew it was an ambush. We spent a rotten boring night for nothing. Our colonel, complete with OBE had botched it.

A few days later one of the paratrooper guards had failed to return after his two-hour guard duty at the shed where I worked. We were afraid that he had been knifed by the thieves. Our gallant colonel roused us from our beds and marched us down with rifles at the slope into the depot. He surrounded my shed and we awaited his command. Fortunately, a major pointed out to him that if we opened fire we would likely shoot one another. I was keeping very low. This major called to me and asked about the exit to the shed. I told him there was only one large door. I suggested we open it and I would go in as I knew the layout very well. He agreed and I slowly entered. I found the missing paratrooper sound asleep on some sacks. I often think of the risk I took, not from thieves but from my colonel. This major did not forget my help.

In Java the locals were killing the Dutch settlers whom they seemed to hate. A detachment of about a dozen men from our unit was ordered to go to Sourabaya for duty. The Major approached me one day and said I was going with him to Java. He told me to pick one corporal and eight sappers who could drive a truck. Of course this was a good move as I was able to pick good men who would all be compatible. We were all set to leave when it was abruptly cancelled. Apparently there was some political difficulty with the Dutch, but as usual we were never informed. All I know is that many people were killed there by the local upstarts who saw their chance when the Japanese withdrew.

My status in the unit had been completely reversed from being the kid with my mates in Burma to being the only man in the unit who had seen active service in Burma.

We worked very hard in Singapore and were very poorly fed. Many of us were malnourished, underweight and tired. I had three spells in the hospital in Singapore. The island was sprayed from the air and mosquitoes were well controlled. As most of the troops had come straight from England we did not get Mepacrine tablets to prevent malaria. After I was in Singapore for about three weeks I came down with malaria as it was no longer being suppressed by Mepacrine. I developed a very high fever and walked to see the local MO, an Indian officer. He complained that I did not salute him. I apologized. He then said I was very sick and must go to the hospital.

The hospital was about one-quarter of a mile along the road and I trudged slowly along. I then had to sign for the sheets for a bed – why I will never know but I complied. I climbed the stairs to a ward on the second floor. By that time I was exhausted and I dropped my admittance form on the nursing sister's desk and headed for an empty bed nearby. I was preparing to get into bed and when the sister who had read the MO's report came rushing up and said, "You are very ill, you mustn't move!"

I was soon under the sheets and requesting more blankets as I was shivering. The other patients were rather alarmed. They were very white and pale as they were just out from the UK and I was very brown. I heard one young lad say, "I hope I don't get what he has." It frightened him.

With treatment I quickly recovered. On another occasion I lost my voice completely. I could not even whisper. I had severe tracheitis of unknown aetiology. I was sent to another hospital. I was put in a large ward with so many patients some were out on the verandah. Many of those outside about ten feet away were men with tuberculosis. It was a terrible arrangement. I discovered that a whole ward was empty except for an officer's wife who was having a baby. We heard her yelling in labour. It seemed that one officer's wife was more important than about thirty sick men.

To add insult to injury we were informed that Lady Mountbatten, the wife of the Supreme Commander, South East Asia, was probably coming to visit us. Immediately we received slippers, Red Cross supplies, writing pads etc. We were told if we were bed patients we must sit to attention when she came. How does one sit to attention? I was pleased she was coming because she had a reputation for raising hell if she found the troops were not being looked after properly. Unfortunately, on the big day she never arrived. I heard later that she chose to visit the 93 Indian General Hospital which was mainly for skin disease and venereal diseases. This was typical of her. Apparently this hospital was in a mess and the top brass never believed she even knew it existed. She raised Hell!

My third spell in hospital was due to a severe ear infection. I was treated with sulphonamides as there was no penicillin available. It was reserved for wounded patients which was OK with me. They even collected the urine from those on penicillin and extracted the drug for reuse. Penicillin is almost all excreted via the urine in humans. This was my first exposure to recycling.

Venereal disease had become a very serious problem in Singapore amongst the troops. In the city there were three worlds – The Great World, the Happy World and the New World. These were amusement parks with cafes, shops, theatres, pin-pong alleys and taxi-dance halls where Chinese girls would dance with you for a ticket which was only about half a Singapore dollar. Of course prostitutes worked their trade in all these establishments. To combat this all girls working there had to be registered and photographed. The idea being if a soldier "got a dose" he was shown the photographs of these girls in order to identify those with the disease and her place of work. This was affectionately called the Family Album.

A task force was recruited to visit these establishments and check surreptitiously on all employees. I was recruited with my friend as he spoke some Malay language. We worked in pairs and could wear civilian clothes if we liked. It was an interesting experience quietly checking on these girls, some of whom were quite nice and friendly and not prostitutes. I still have a photograph given to me by a lovely young Chinese girl. Unfortunately, one prostitute recognized my mate one evening and she yelled 'Picket Men' which was the name given to our squad. All hell broke loose with irate prostitutes as we quickly retreated. We had some fun at that job.

The Army made it possible for soldiers to take the equivalent of the English GCE exam for high school students. They ran courses on pre-vocational training in the evenings in the city. One day they were short of a maths teacher and my Major friend had looked up my records and saw that I had completed my first year in engineering at Glasgow University when I was 17 years old. I was summoned and asked to be a maths teacher. I explained I had forgotten much of my mathematics and was not prepared. I was immediately given time off plus books to study. I tried hard to get out of it but as it was only until the Army Education Corps took over, I finally agreed. I asked why one of the many officers in our unit could not do the job. I was told one of our lieutenants would be in my class. I knew this lieutenant well. He was a little Jewish man who received terrible treatment from our colonel. He was a decent guy who had no desire to be a soldier. Later we became friends and we went into the city together in civilian clothes.

I knew our CO was a bastard but never realized he was so rotten to his junior officers. To add to our miserable life they started to give military training on Saturday mornings. I managed to get out of that, except for one morning when I had to lecture and demonstrate on mines, demolitions and booby-traps. You would think all these hearty types from Sandhurst would have been full of this stuff and would be able to do the job. I did the job my way, and was told it was the best attended class so far. I began by telling them how I made my first little bomb, when I was 16, at high school. I used the

same ingredients as the IRA, and they were all commonly
available chemicals. Of course I did not mention the IRA, I
substituted the Scottish Nationalists. This caused quite a stir
and later some officers actually questioned me about my lecture.
I just said I did this to get their attention. It certainly worked
and my lecture was a success.

I think, since there was a risk of mutiny over our poor food
and heavy duties, the officers did not feel safe. At Kluang in
Malaya there was full scale mutiny by the Paratroop Regiment
and the Devonshire Regiment was sent to quell it. Sure enough
we had a small mutiny one morning before marching to work.
We then got less guard duty and better food. The GOC's
cook was a London chef and he was sent to take over our
cook-house.

We had one small slightly built sapper who was rather an
introvert and a loner in our unit. There was some concern
over his mental state and it was decided to send him to Penang,
an island off the north west coast of Malaya, where there was
a newly opened leave centre for British troops. It was thought
undesirable to send him alone and he was asked if he had any
mates. He mentioned my name as I had befriended him in
the past.

I was lucky as they sent me on two week's leave with him
to Penang. We got on just fine. He told me his parents ran a
pub in London and never had much time for him, but gave
him gifts. It was a paradox. I came from a family of twelve
children and he was a lonely only child. We hit it off and
enjoyed our leave.

While on Penang Island I met a rich Chinese merchant who
had two very nice daughters and two wives. He invited me
to his country home as he liked to talk about the Japanese.

Of course, I was mainly interested in his daughters. He introduced his small son to me with great pride then merely mentioned his two wives and two daughters, just as if he also had a dog.

His home was luxurious. We sat at a round dinner table and he explained the Chinese table had no head. His number one wife stood behind his chair, while number two wife stood behind my chair and her son sat at my left. This was quite an experience. The various courses of the meal kept coming and if I did not like one it was quickly removed by number two wife and replaced by the next course. We drank rice wine and I was told to drink up when my host drank – he called this Yamsing. Then number two wife would quickly refill my glass. Oh well, when in Rome do as the Romans do, I enjoyed my Chinese dinner and my host was very gracious and interesting. He puzzled over my dislike at being called English, but he soon learned we Scots were a much different race.

Singapore was quite a pleasant place to be, compared to Burma and Malaya. However, as the white colonial types who had fled to England before the Japanese arrived, began to filter back, things changed. Their clubs reopened and were out of bounds to army personnel except for commissioned officers. There was one particular club – The Orchard Club – which refused us entry. It seems we were good enough to fight the Nips to restore their rubber plantations and tin mines etc. but were quite unfit to sit in the same restaurant with them.

One evening a group of paratroopers descended on the club and would not be denied entry. The MPs were called and later the Malay police. A big fight ensued which the "red-berets" won and they trashed the place. They were moved to Kluang in Malaya where they eventually mutinied.

It was not difficult to perceive that Malaya and Singapore would soon rid themselves of these types. The war had changed many things and attitudes. I was disgusted with these colonial types. They got what they deserved. The Hume Pipe Company, a Dutch firm, offered me a job out there but I declined the offer with good reason. Anyway, by now my sights were set on going back to Glasgow University.

At that time the population of Singapore was about one million on a small island. They were mainly Chinese with some Indians, mostly Tamils from South India and a small percentage of Eurasians who were half Chinese and half European. The latter group were rather isolated socially but very nice people. The Chinese were very industrious and progressive. It is not hard to see how Singapore advanced into the bustling prosperous city it became.

As for the Japanese POWs they all were sent home before me. When I arrived in Singapore from Burma, I really hated the Nips. Not so much the result of my experiences in Burma but their despicable treatment of our POWs on the Burma-Siam railway. Gradually, as I got to know individual Japanese soldiers, I realized they were little different from me, except their officers had almighty power over them and treated them quite brutally. I could never bring myself to like the Japanese officer class. They were well educated which made their behaviour all the more inexcusable. Their military code was no excuse. They were apart from humanity. Unfortunately, I was not allowed to beat them up or abuse them. My only weapon was to make them lose face in front of everyone, especially the Chinese.

The Japanese had great difficulty with the letter L in English. I used to ask them to say lollipop for my amusement. They also had difficulty with the F sound. I remember their interpreter asking me politely "Please, Master, British soldiers, all time hocking in conversation. What is hocking, I cannot find in dictionary."

I replied, "No wonder you lost the hocking war." He still did not understand so I made a gesture with my finger and said syco, syco. At last he understood and laughed. I did not need to draw him a picture.

The Japanese soldiers, even POWs, were very diligent and hard-working and clean. I had seen them in action and their attacking and retreating manoeuvres could not be faulted. I am not surprised that Japan today is a prosperous and progressive nation. Despite this, I believe the British soldier was superior. He was much less reliant on his officers and was more resourceful when left on his own. Without orders he could be relied upon to fight well, whether advancing or retreating. He protected and assisted his comrades at all times. He did lots of moaning about his circumstances but always made the best of it. These were qualities which were inherent and quite unrelated to his military training. These were also attributes which served them well in the jungle warfare of the Burma campaign.

After two years in Singapore I was in very poor physical condition due to poor nutrition and overwork in the equatorial heat. At last my demob number came up and I was on my way home in another troop ship. On this occasion 1 travelled in sergeants' quarters with bunk beds and decent food. We played solo whist most of the way home. In fact we were still playing when the ship was about to dock at Liverpool. At Port Said at the north end of the Suez Canal, we anchored to take on water and supplies. The Egyptian bum boats came alongside to sell fruit and handbags. I had no Egyptian money but I bartered an army blanket via the port hole for a nice embossed leather handbag for my old mother. I was soon copied. Then the ship's tanoid announced anyone selling blankets to the Arabs would be court-martialled.

On arrival at Liverpool, many relatives had gathered near the dockside. The troops used empty fifty-cigarette tins to throw messages to their relatives on the dock. The "red-caps" tried to intercept these tins – God alone knows why. Of course, this incited the troops to pelt the "red-caps" with anything handy. More tanoid messages followed. We docked during the night and the lazy Liverpool dockers refused to unload our kit bags from the hold. Squads of weary soldiers were detailed to do this work. The lazy dockers waited for the army gear to be removed, then they demanded hot cocoa before they would begin work on the cargo. They came alongside the ship to each port hole asking for spare tunics or greatcoats. One happened to ask a big burly soldier who had been pulled out of his bed to unload our kit bags. He was incensed and pulled the docker by the head through the port hole, all the time questioning his parentage and idle disposition. It was not really a warm welcome to our native land.

We were soon disembarked and sent by train to York to be demobbed. There we had a four-hour wait to allow some troops from Germany to go through before us. By the time we had our turn all the best of the civilian clothes had gone. We were still the Forgotten Army!

Eventually, I boarded the train for Scotland with another sergeant from Glasgow. The train was packed but we found a compartment with two spare seats. We did not notice that the passengers were all women. One kindly old Glasgow lady opposite me inquired about our journey – thirty days on a cramped troop ship after three years in the Far East. She was obviously glad we were going home and gave us what must have been her sweet ration.

All went well until a ticket inspector entered to check his passengers. Immediately, a crusty old lady in one corner complained in a very la-di-da voice that this was a ladies' compartment and we had no right to be here. Before we could move the old Glasgow lady let rip at the complainer. She told her she should be ashamed of her behaviour to these poor returning servicemen. At one time I thought she was going to eject the toffee-nosed old lady. We offered to leave but the others would not hear of it. The inspector retreated hastily and peace was restored. It was not exactly a warm welcome to England.

After a dismal journey I was back in my hometown and carrying my kitbag up the same street on which I had walked every day to school. My old mother was shocked at my poor state, but I was home, finally home, and a civilian again after almost four long years. I had just graduated from the world's best finishing school. I had been exposed to many other races and cultures – American, Indian, Nepalese, Burmese, Malay, African, Chinese and Japanese. I had learned a great deal about life and death. Having been born and raised in a large family of twelve children, the everyday army life was not the traumatic experience it was to most wartime soldiers. My army service had damaged me physically but not mentally.

CHAPTER 3

Disaster

It was a strange experience to return to a home that was relatively quiet with only my old parents in residence. Most of my elder brothers and sisters had all been married and installed in their own homes. My eldest brother was still serving in the RAF and one sister had married and gone to Canada. My twin brother was still awaiting demob in Austria as he had joined the army later than me.

I had not had a proper sleep for days and was very tired. I can well recall having my own room for the first time in my life. I crawled into an old but comfortable bed with hand-washed sheets specially prepared by my old mother. It was sheer luxury and I vowed never to leave home again.

Food was still scarce in Britain and strictly rationed. Currants and raisins were almost unobtainable but my old mother had managed to find some and kept them for my return to make a rice pudding as I used to enjoy that. I never let her know how terrible my diet had been – rice twice per day with the Indian soldiers – and every day. Bravely I ate the rice pudding which was meant as a special treat. It was the least I could do. I was very thin and tired but I explained that now I was home I would soon pick up in condition.

After a few weeks I took a job on a local dairy farm. I had learned that as a returning veteran I could apply for a government scholarship (FET which meant Further Education and Training Grant). This was quite generous and paid all university fees and expenses, plus a good living allowance. I had always wanted to take veterinary medicine and surgery but could never afford a five year course of this type. Now it all seemed possible and I was determined to apply and I knew ex-servicemen would get preference when filling the limited number of places (30) at Glasgow University. My job on the farm would also be looked upon with favour by a selection committee.

All went well on the farm. Up at 5 am and finished at 6 pm but with lots of good food, cream, fresh eggs and bacon etc. We had a huge side of a large pig hanging from the farm kitchen ceiling and you just sliced off what you wanted for breakfast.

I studied in the evening by the light of a paraffin lamp and I was content. I was however still very thin and easily tired and was not making much of a recovery. My big day eventually came and I was accepted for a place at Glasgow Veterinary School starting on 5 October 1948. I had had a visit from a lady from Edinburgh about my FET grant. She drove right on to the farm and seemed impressed so I was given a generous allowance. I could afford to stay in lodgings in Glasgow near college and save four hours per day of valuable study time as my home was about a ninety-minute journey from the college.

I found lodgings in Glasgow five minutes from the college and everything was going according to plan. I was rather startled on my first day of classes. I was the oldest student and many were straight out of high school. I had left school six years before. This merely spurred me on to work hard. My only concern was my health. I developed a very bad cold which never seemed to subside. After about two months of damp, cold Glasgow winter weather I became quite sick. I suddenly noticed blood stains in the mucus I coughed up and I soon deduced that it was not just a bad cough and cold. I visited my doctor and then went to the Western Infirmary close to the university to see a chest physician. It was soon confirmed that I had active pulmonary tuberculosis and must return home at once. I believe it was the worst day of my life to have to tell my old mother my bad news. After all the long years of wartime service in which five sons, two daughters and four sons-in-law had all miraculously returned safely, I now had to give her such tragic news.

In those days pulmonary tuberculosis was like a death sentence – a slow death sentence. There were no effective drugs and bed rest and fresh air in a sanatorium, generally in an isolated location, were the accepted methods of treatment. I cast my mind back to my army service in the Far East. First the terrible conditions in Burma, poor nutrition and exhaustion. Then my service in Singapore with long hours of work in the tropical sun – almost right on the equator, with again poor nutrition.

I also recalled one of these three spells in hospital in Singapore during which I was in bed about ten feet apart from tuberculosis patients on the hospital verandah. Their utensils etc. were frequently mixed up with our own.

The medical officer on my ward at that time was an army lady doctor and was really nice and caring, but obviously had little say in the matter. In any case, I was sure that my infection took place right there in hospital under ideal conditions for such a contagious disease to be spread. I believe it was criminal and unethical for this state of affairs to exist. When I applied for a War Pension I explained the situation to the Appeal Board, but they remained silent and unresponsive. They were obviously not about to rock the boat and lose a nice well paid job. They awarded me a one hundred per cent war disablement pension.

Within a few days of January 1949, I was transported by ambulance about thirty-five miles away to a large sanatorium up in the Ochil Hills. My poor mother was devastated but I assured her I would return.

The hospital was a large two-storey sandstone mansion house with a nice big lawn along the front. It was an impressive building from the outside and obviously had been the residence of a very wealthy family. Unfortunately, the interior was very spartan. The rooms all faced the front and housed two to three patients, except for some very large rooms which held ten to twelve beds. The floors were bare wood and the beds were old, single, army-style iron frames with old mattresses. Each patient had a small locker and a wooden tray off which to eat meals. There were no bed lights, no curtains, no fixtures and no carpets. Radios were the patients' own property. The only redeeming feature was the view over the hills. The nearest village was about three miles away and it was all down hill, so we could see some signs of civilisation. There were no nurses, only two male orderlies for the men.

The superintendent was a doctor who had been given the job, because he himself had the disease, although not very severely. He was nicknamed "Big Mac" which had no connection with hamburgers. He had another doctor to assist him who was an old retired Royal Navy Commander. He was a gentlemanly old man but not very adept at taking blood samples. Fortunately, his wife was much younger, and also a physician, and she always performed this monthly task on all patients (about one hundred). We had one nursing sister for the women's quarters on the second floor and another sister for the men. In addition there was one night sister for everyone. The matron performed most of the administration and her assistant dished out the meals for both bed patients and those able to go to the mess hall. Maids and cleaners were employed from the nearby village.

We had a two-hour visiting period in the afternoon on Wednesday, Saturday and Sunday and a special bus ran from Stirling and also from Dumferline. For my visitors that meant about four hours travelling time plus two hours visiting time. This meant I would get visitors one day per week and sometimes once every two weeks. This did not bother me too much as I had been used to being away for years at a time in the army.

The treatment was mainly bed rest, fresh air and good food. The latter was a joke. Britain was still very short of food and almost everything was rationed. The meals were very poor – porridge and toast for breakfast – maybe one egg per week. Soup for lunch and a main course for dinner, mostly of poor cheap cuts of meat. We were not allowed to have tea or coffee between times but, of course, we had a few ex-servicemen and we quickly acquired small electric stoves to make our own. It was always a challenge to beat the system, just like in the army.

I was very fortunate as my farmer friends sent fresh eggs, fresh hand-churned butter and even bacon. Thank God for the food parcels – we called them Red Cross parcels, as sent to POWs.

We had an orderly take our temperature and pulse every morning and evening. We also all had a small sputum bottle, like a ladies' perfume bottle, with disinfectant instead of perfume. The disease caused sporadic coughing and retching which was as they say, "productive", and lumps of sputum were brought up from the bronchial tree and deposited in these bottles. You received a clean sterile one every morning.

I remember well having to walk past the front of the building late one evening and I listened to the nocturnal chorus of coughing and retching coming sporadically from all areas of the hospital. It was the same in the morning – our own special dawn chorus. I could even identify some of the coughers.

My first few days as a bed patient were spent beside a room-mate who was very sick indeed. He was very thin and pale and extremely weak. I helped him all I could and we were good friends. Unfortunately, he suddenly gulped after a severe bout of coughing and keeled over the side of his bed with blood gushing over the wooden floor. He was choking on his own blood and I rushed out of bed to try to help him breath. It was a horrible mess as most of the blood in his body seemed to cover the floor like a red carpet. I rang for help but it was so sudden and too late. He died in my hands.

Our nursing sister finally came and rudely ordered me out of the room. From that time I had a permanent dislike of that woman. I had seen a few horrible scenes in Burma, where badly wounded soldiers bled to death but there it merely soaked into the ground and was much less alarming than with this poor lad. The body was moved at night to the morgue, as was the custom, so that patients did not see it. I was moved to another room and given clean pyjamas and told to say nothing to other patients. This was typical of the childish way we were treated.

Several patients appeared to be in need of constant bed rest. I was not too bad, relatively speaking, so I was moved out of the main building to some huts which were about 200 yards away. They were really brick buildings which housed about ten men on either side of central toilets and washing facilities. This made me quite happy as I had more company and could walk to the main building dining room for my meals. We had a few ex-service men among the patients which imparted a good sense of comradeship and life was much more interesting. We spent a lot of time bypassing the many stupid rules. In a way it was like being back in the army. The patients ran a big part of the organization. One man acted as postman, another collected pensions and sick benefit allowances and travelled daily to the village and cashed them for the inmates. Some of us would fill porcelain hot water bottles for bed patients in the main block. They were necessary as it was very cold with very little heating. Woman and men were of course separated, except for any social events or when filling these water bottles from a common washroom where fraternization was possible. There was never a shortage of volunteers for this task. Hormones are powerful little compounds! You would be surprised just how long it took to fill these bottles, much to the annoyance of the matron.

The old doctor was Henry — I am sure this was a nickname as his surname was Ford; the Scots are very adept at applying nicknames to individuals. Just as in the Army anyone called Whyte was automatically called Chalky White. Warren became Bunny, Green became Pea, Clark became Nobby and so on. Henry found out I had been a veterinary student — only for about two months, and he asked me to assist him every month when blood was taken from every patient for BSR (blood sedimentation rate). Blood samples were sucked into a graduated glass tube and were held vertically in a stand. The red cells fell to the bottom and the rate of fall was measured after one hour and recorded. This is a very general indication of health of the patient. Rates ranged from a few millimetres up to the whole length of the measure over one hour. The higher the rate of fall the poorer the health of the patient. Henry was useless at intravenous work so his wife took the samples and I did the rest. This meant going round the whole hospital to all bed patients. I believe I was the only male patient who had ever been in the women's rooms. I think I was more self-conscious than any of the women patients, but at least I was being useful.

I later graduated to doing dispensary work and I made up all the prescriptions for coughs etc. for all the patients and also delivered them. I got lots of ribbing from my mates and of course I exaggerated a bit just for fun. I did not mind the work although I often think I should have been supervised as some of the drugs were quite toxic and required accurate dispensing. I often wondered just how these doctors passed their time. The Chief of the hospital was seen about once or twice a week when he visited our hut during rest hour which was from two to three o'clock and meant mandatory bed rest. He would stand at the end of the hut and ask how you were. He was too idle to walk to each bed and look clinically at each patient. I though then if a veterinarian were to stand at the end of a cow shed to examine animals for health he would not have lasted very long.

I evoked the Chief's ire one day by asking if he had received any streptomycin for treatment. He was very annoyed and said I should not worry about that. I replied that I read where it was being used in bull's semen for artificial insemination to control infections such as vibriosis and brucellosis. I believe it was eventually tried in tuberculosis treatment. I am afraid this medical dynamo was not amused and thereafter was always sarcastic or condescending towards me. This did not bother me unduly as I had been dealing with incompetent army officers for years.

My condition was stable but not improving. It was decided to collapse my right lung as it was badly affected and required rest to allow healing. I had a cavity in my right apex which meant that there was considerable damage and always the risk of haemorrhage if a major vessel eroded. I was never consulted of course, merely wheeled into the operating room and a large bore needle was thrust between my middle ribs as I lay on my left side. Air was then siphoned into my right chest cavity and my right lung would be partially deflated. Each week I received a refill of air, just like a tire. The process was carried out weekly for about a year. I never knew if it was being beneficial or not. As we said in the army, I was a mushroom – i.e. being fed on horse manure and kept in the dark.

Big Mac was no help. He refused any information on my progress or lack of it, which suggested to me the whole procedure was not beneficial. After about ten months he spoke of having a big thoracoplastic operation done on me in Dundee by a special surgeon. I knew the procedure was to cut out sections of my right ribs from the rear so that my chest would collapse permanently and flatten my right lung. This was a drastic step to take and one which would leave me with a lowered right shoulder and badly deformed chest, not to mention loss of breath. I told him I would like another independent opinion on this drastic step. He was furious and stamped out of the room without reply. Many years later on reflection I seriously questioned his motives. He was a vindictive man and not too competent.

Soon I was a "marked man" and life was made difficult for me. One nursing sister was very belligerent towards me and once said I would have to clean all the brass work – like a child being punished. I replied I would begin with her neck. During all my stay over one year in this hospital I never received a single visit from the War Pensions Authorities, even though there were about ten war pensioners in the hospital.

Despite my troubles I was far from being the poorest patient in the hospital. There were a few men and women with no relatives or visitors, no money and little hope. I befriended a poor lad who had no possessions except for a night shirt and no income at all. He was bedfast yet surprisingly cheerful and always pleasant to me. I used to take him the daily newspaper as he had no money to buy one. Sometimes I would put a pound note inside and would say, "There is an interesting article on page three, Bill." In this way no one else knew I was giving him money. I also would take him a few home baked goodies as my sisters and sister-in-law were expert bakers and sent me treats regularly.

I knew a girl upstairs who, also, was all alone in the world with little hope of ever leaving the hospital alive. I had to get one of the maids to take her some goodies and money. The maid told me she was quite overwhelmed at the gifts. It made me feel good but also very humble.

When I went around with the lady doctor each month to take the blood sample she was always so grateful. I believe the lady doctor knew my secret but being the fine gracious lady that she was she never made any comment. What a difference from Big Mac!

In two cases both father and daughter were patients in

hospital and also two brothers. With poor overcrowded housing in some poor areas of Scotland, it was not surprising. The severe wartime food rationing was also a factor.

As the months rolled on it became obvious to me that I would never make progress in the hospital with the attitude 'Big Mac' and his subservient sister had towards me. I therefore requested to see the tuberculosis doctor for Stirlingshire. He was a very active man and a true Scot. He finally visited the hospital and I asked old Henry who was with him if I could talk to him privately. I got my request and within the hour I had unburdened my troubles to him. I told him I intended to leave and return home. He assured me I would be taken care of by himself and perhaps he would get me into another hospital. I consequently packed up one Sunday afternoon and returned with one of my mate's parents in their car to within ten miles of my home. They fed me at their home and I took the bus the rest of the way. On reflection it was a brave move, but as it turned out a good one.

I had my own room at home with plenty of fresh air and my mother's cooking. I travelled into Stirling every Wednesday for a refill of air for my chest, administered by the same doctor I had talked to at the hospital. He proved to be a really good doctor and very sympathetic and understanding. Later he became the first Scottish Nationalist MP in Parliament. He suspected that my artificial pneumothorax, as it was called, was ineffective. He sent me to Ruchill Hospital in Glasgow where they had a look inside my chest at my right lung. I heard them say, "My God, look at all these adhesions, like guy ropes, these ought to have been cut long ago. No wonder this is not working." They later told me it was too late to cut them now and they would let my lung inflate. When I asked about the thoracoplastic operation they said definitely no! They said it was contra-indicated.

I knew now my suspicions were well founded about Big Mac. As my lung was allowed to inflate I got a pleural effusion which was fluid around the outside of my lung in the chest cavity. This was uncomfortable but soon dissipated. I took great care of myself at home and I was feeling better for the first time in years. I improved in condition and became heavier. I knew I was on the mend and had cheated death!

My doctor in Stirling was always helpful and encouraged me. Eventually as the time came for the start of a new college year I asked him if I could return to my studies. He looked at me hard and long then said, "Will you promise me to look after your health and come and see me every term?" Of course I agreed heartily. As an added safeguard he arranged to have my right phrenic nerve crushed to paralyse the right side of my diaphragm and help rest my right lung. I was operated on a Saturday morning in Stirling and went to Glasgow University on the Tuesday morning, 5 October 1950, to restart my first year of study with the stitches still in my neck.

My fellow students were all very young, age 19 and I was 25 years old, and nine years out of high school. When they inquired about my neck I just said a hen kicked me.

My doctor was a great encouragement to me and even came into his office on a Saturday morning to check me over. I owe him a great debt for his confidence in me and his medical care.

My old professor at the Glasgow Veterinary School was a pillar of strength for me. He was a very respected man in the veterinary profession, globally. When I told him of my previous difficulties he would say, "Put it down to experience. Some day you will look back on it all with amusement." He offered

me a post at the college a short time before my final exams.
I recall his exact words; "Mr. MacKay, there is a crib for you
here if you want it." I had my sights set on a postgraduate
degree, then a post in the Government Veterinary Investigation
Service, so I declined. He was, as always, gracious and encouraged me to proceed with my plans. I thanked him for all his
confidence in me and said I would do my best to uphold the
honour of my veterinary school. Later the Queen made him
Sir William Weipers, a well-deserved accolade.

Later in life when I reminisced on my hospital days, I often
admired the dedication of some of the staff at the sanatorium.
To live and work in such an isolated place and perform such
unpleasant duties required tremendous dedication with very
poor reward. Nursing sisters, orderlies and even maids provided
a service to these unfortunate patients, which for some of the
patients was their last experience before death. I used to
compare them to the stretcher-bearers and medics in the
forward areas in the Burma Campaign. They were unsung
heroes, always under great personal risk.

Unfortunately, all professional staff were not in this category.
Our nursing sister looked more like a hooker than a nurse.
Her skirt was always above her knees and her not too pleasant
face well enamelled with make-up − even a large pimple, or
as we say in Scotland, a plook was made up. Naturally, she
worked only in the men's ward. The superintendent at the
hospital or hospital chief was not very visible. I cannot recall
him ever putting a stethoscópe on my chest. As for old "Henry"
he screened all patients every week before they had refills of
air, i.e. artificial pneumothorax patients, or as we called them
A-P patients. His sight was not good and when he did the air
refills he had to ask the sister what the reading was on the

manometer. He was a real gentleman and was always very appreciative of the help I gave him.

Our male orderly was a very conscientious worker. He recorded our temperature and pulse twice daily. He always had difficulty with my pulse and swore it was my fault. I never understood why. If you received any eggs from your visitors he would inscribe them with your name in the evening, for breakfast the next morning. Thank God for my farming friends.

The local Church of Scotland minister sometimes paid us a visit from the village. He was a nice man and very interested in any stories we had to tell. He even wanted me to write something for him to publish. I often regret I did not do this when all was so fresh and real in my mind. Through him, I received a visit from the local veterinarian from the village. He brought me a nice book on animals. Later, in my fourth year at college, I spent some time in his country practice as a student. He was a very busy man working seven days per week, and I was grateful for his visit. All in all my stay in the sanatorium for a whole year was a memorable experience. They say adversity brings out the best or worst in people. Certainly there were a number of very courageous patients and many never left the place alive. It was a very humbling experience for me.

Life at home after leaving the hospital was much happier and I took great care of my health and did everything I could to speed recovery. It was sometime before my old mother was assured that I would recover. I did my best to show her I would soon be fit to return to veterinary school.

Everyone was not so nice to me. One old neighbour in our street was extremely nosy. She approached me one day in the street and stood about ten feet away with the backs of her hand over her mouth. She then asked how I was and proceeded to inquire if I was receiving any money. I assured her I was getting a war disablement pension. She immediately asked how much and I replied twenty-five pounds per week. In actual fact I received one hundred per cent pension amounting to two pounds and twelve shillings per week which was far less than the minimum wage in Scotland at that time. She gasped and said that was a big pension. I replied, yes but of course it may not be for very long, as it was cut off at death. I then pulled out my handkerchief and held it over my mouth and said I needed to cough. She ran off, out of my way.

In those days there were no anti-tubercular drugs and the disease was like the plague. You were shunned in public if people knew your condition. I often think of the present day Aids infection and compare it to tuberculosis. I believe people are much more tolerant of Aids sufferers than they were of me, yet my disease was the result of very long and arduous military service and no fault of mine. This is difficult to understand. Perhaps if I had lost an arm or a leg in combat I would have received much better acceptance and sympathy.

I had seen lepers in a leper colony. Everyone avoided them as unclean. The bacterium which causes leprosy is *Mycobacterium leprae* while my infection was with *Mycobacterium tuberculosis var hominis*, i.e. the same family of bacteria but with different clinical effects. With *Mycobacterium tuberculosis* there are three forms, human, bovine (or mammalian) and avian. All produced different syndromes of disease which varies with the host species. Later as a veterinarian working in pathology, I would ironically become expert in their diagnosis and differentiations. This was a subject in which I would acquire expert knowledge. My experience with this disease had some useful aspects.

My long stay in the hospital gave me lots of time to think. In my small country town, everyone knew everyone and all their business. I decided that I would keep my medical history to myself when I went to the Glasgow Veterinary School. Of course there was always a busybody and a student in my class wanted to know about the scar on my neck from the phrenic crush. I said I had been in a big fight in the NAAFI queue (the soldier's canteen). He was not convinced and pressed me along with some others for an explanation. I gave them their request. I described how I had been isolated in a forward position in the jungle by a rapid Japanese advance. Several Nips came at me with their long bayonets and I was trapped. I then remained silent and after a few moments they demanded to know what else happened. I just said "They killed me". I was never bothered by them again!

My hospital experience had made me very determined and self-reliant. I had too much at stake so I worked very diligently. I had one big advantage – I had developed natural cunning as my old training sergeant had advised. One of my young classmates once complained that I was a fly guy which in Scotland meant shrewd or quick-thinking. I repeated that there was nothing to prevent him being likewise.

Every man is born with a certain amount of natural cunning, it is up to the individual to develop it. This was a characteristic I had cultivated right from my early army days and one which stood me in good stead in veterinary work where you are very dependent on your own observations and your ability to assess the true history of the animal from the owner's remarks. Sick animals never disguise their condition and never tell you lies.

CHAPTER 4

Student Days

After years of army life, when all my thinking was done
for me, then in the hospital where I was discouraged
severely for thinking for myself, life as a first year veterinary
student was a complete and pleasant change of life-style. I was
challenged to compete with much younger and well educated
colleagues. Life was exciting and strenuous. Although I was
much older, I had a good rapport with my younger classmates.
Student life can be hard, but always interesting. Practical jokes
and amusement are an accepted part of the course. They act
like a safety value and are socially acceptable. When I am asked
about my student days, I invariable recall the pranks and jokes
we played on our lecturers and classmates. Our lecturers were
by and large very tolerant and even on odd occasions
participated. Of course, there were the odd exceptions who
disapproved, and as a consequence their lives were made hell
by the students at every opportunity. Needless to say, these
stuffed shirts were not the best at conveying knowledge. We
had a chemistry lecturer from Glasgow, who was typical of
the local population – very sharp and witty, but a very good
teacher. If someone made a smart remark, he would recognize
it and say, "If you had any more wit you would be a half-wit"
to loud cheers. I recall one day a smart guy in our class gave
a stupid response to his questions. He looked at him and said,
"If you had a brain you would be dangerous, or it would be
lonely."

Chemistry was the subject which was used to eliminate students in the first year, who were unlikely to make it academically through the five year course. This was a wise and necessary ploy to avoid scarce places being occupied by students who would take far too long to graduate, if ever. I made sure I knew my chemistry.

We had several lecturers for zoology, one of whom had difficulty with the "th" sound; he referred to "teef". Of course, we went out of our way to ask questions about teeth just to cause him embarrassment. In every class there are a few "jokers". We had an Englishman who excelled in this art. One afternoon we had live narcotized snails for dissection in the laboratory. He boasted he would eat one for a quid (£1). We very quickly had a whip around the class and collected the required sum of money. By this time the word had gone out and some other lecturers including the professor had come to watch. The student thanked everyone for the contributions, then stood up and gulped down the snail, shell and all, to great applause.

We had a young female lecturer for genetics. Silk stockings were still very scarce and she had bare legs which were very hairy. One cruel student asked her if there was a gene for hairy legs. No one was safe or sacred. We had a young student from a wealthy family who supplied him with a new MG sports car. It had a little dickie seat in the back. Along with another joker they collected a big friendly shaggy collie dog from an adjacent street in Glasgow in his MG. They brought it into the zoology lecture theatre, which was like a steep amphitheatre, with narrow benches in front of the seats. The lecturer was on a raised platform facing the middle level of the class. They placed the dog between them, sitting up like a student with a book in front of it. Our lecturer deliberated for about ten minutes before he noticed the dog as it began to pant. He fell back towards the blackboard and said, "Whose is the dog?" Of course we all looked around saying, "what dog?" He then asked someone to remove it, but we all appeared confused. He finally removed it himself, carrying it over his shoulder to great cheers. Before his next lecture I saw him poke his nose through the small door at the top of the lecturer room, to make sure there were no new surprises. At the start of his lecture some joker told him there was a dog in here without a collar. He was startled and looked all around the class. Then someone pointed to a big student who had an open neck shirt and of course no collar. I could well understand why lecturers did not relish the idea of taking the veterinary classes. For all our practical jokes he proved to be a very able lecturer and was well liked by us.

Our physics lecturer was a real stuffed shirt. I recall when he announced that at next day's lecture we would go on to sound. The next day as soon as he said, "Today we will start sound," all hell broke loose – bells, whistles, alarm clocks and even a trumpet filled the lecture theatre. He was not amused – no sense of humour.

In my second year we had a little Austrian who gave some lectures on histology. He was about five feet tall and very Teutonic – "The best books on this subject are in German of course", which brought on a unanimous "Zieg Heil" from the students. He was so small he required a wooden box to stand on, while lecturing in a room which had a level floor. He insisted routinely on calling the roll before every lecture, even when we had two consecutive lectures. His English was poor and he had difficulty with some of the names, e.g., Noble was pronounced "No ball", to which everyone said – "Oh shame" or "pity". He never did catch on. One day a student put an alarm clock in his box and as he lectured it went off. He jumped off the box and fled the room.

On another occasion we removed his box and hid it. He brought in the senior lecturer who asked the class who had taken the box. We all pointed to a small inoffensive meek student. The senior lecturer carried on the joke and with a straight face asked the small student what he had done with the box. He of course denied all knowledge of it. It was like a pantomime – I could have sold tickets for the show.

When we were studying liver histology in the laboratory he approached me and looked down my microscope and said, "Do not confuse the sinuses of Lushka with the spaces of Rockitanski Ashcoff."

I replied, "I would never do that."

The lecturer was of little use in conveying knowledge to students. He had a habit of coming round the laboratory class and asking questions. I forestalled him one day by asking him to solve a problem for me. If a chicken had its trachea (wind pipe) blocked and broke its leg, could it still breathe? As you know chicken leg bones have cavities in them and there are air sacs in the body cavity, which render them more buoyant. This ploy worked a treat and he set off to consult the books as he did not want to lose face in front of the students. We were allowed to get on with our lab work for a few days.

In our anatomy class we had a lady junior lecturer who was extremely boring and merely repeated word for word from a textbook, except her every phrase was preceded by "Ah um". We asked her "What was an Ah um?" She did not get our message. We then counted the "Ah ums" and when she reached fifty we all cheered, much to her consternation. We explained that she was lecturing at so many "Ah ums" to the minute and no one knew what they were! One day she was lecturing on the pelvis of the cow and one bored student at the back of the class had a bovine anatomical pelvic specimen with an elastic band stretched over the pelvic bones, on which he played a tune. She finally asked him to come down to the front of the class and bring his organ with him. There followed numerous "Ohs and ahs" and howls from the class, which turned her cheeks a bright red, as the comments kept coming. She was a very self-assured lady but something of a parrot learner. One day my little syndicate for anatomy practice, was working on dissecting a bovine carcass. We decided to test her knowledge. We passed a thin piece of white string, several times through red muscle, then carefully placed it in the carcass to resemble a nerve. We then asked her to identify this nerve. She quickly pronounced on it as a branch of the vagus nerve. We argued a little but she would not be swayed from her opinion. We then removed it and let her see it was merely a piece of string. She took the joke poorly.

For someone who spends five years in Glasgow, it would be impossible not to encounter the Glasgow sense of humour. The Glaswegians are well known for their quick wit and down to earth demeanour. I remember watching an amateur boxing match in the Kelvin Hall Glasgow, between Scotland and England. The English lad was continually being warned by the referee, for butting his opponent with his head. When he persisted he was warned again, an irate fan yelled "Put a glove on it ref." Student dances at the Glasgow Veterinary School on Saturday nights were always great fun. The girls from various colleges e.g The Domestic Science School – nicknamed the

'Dough' school, were always phoning the students rec-room for tickets to these dances, I remember two girls were told to pick up their tickets at the door from the student organizer, who was a very serious-minded student. However, they were told that it was a fancy dress ball and no one would be admitted unless in fancy dress. When they arrived in fancy dress and found everyone in casual attire, they were furious and our serious minded organizer had to flee.

Even the Glasgow kids had a cheeky sense of humour. In Glasgow before the advent of cellular phones and police cars with two-way radio, the police had red police boxes, which were mainly small communication centres situated at strategic points in the city. The Glasgow police were very efficient and the michevious youngsters around the college required constant supervision. I recall one cheeky errant boy about 8 years old was being troublesome, and the policeman shut him up in the police box for about one hour. When he released him he ran off about 100 yards then yelled, 'Ha Ha! I ate your piece (lunch). Sure enough he had eaten a large ham and egg sandwich, which was for the policeman's lunch. We felt amused but sorry about the man's lunch, so we offered to get him a sandwich from our college canteen kitchen. We quickly acquired this and offered it to the policeman. He was still a bit apprehensive of our gift, but we offered to let him talk to the canteen cook who had prepared it. Finally all was well. After all the Glasgow police treated us with a great deal of tolerance especially on Charities Day in Glasgow when the students in fancy dress, raise money for the local hospitals etc. These days were always great fun.

We always had a few overseas students in every year. One year we had a wealthy student named 'Indian Joe'. He drank a fair amount. He once came to our Saturday night dance in the College and was drinking heavily. Some students obtained a few white mice from the College pathology laboratory. They stained these mice a bright pink colour with carbol-fuchsin, a red stain used in the laboratory. These red mice were released into his Ford Pilot car. When he eventually went to drive home, they ran around his steering wheel and dashboard. He staggered back into the college and sat head down and said "I will never drink again" – and for a while he did not!

All this was great fun and a welcome release from endless days of intensive study. Glasgow humour was a great tonic for weary students.

We had a senior lecturer in medicine who was very academic and mustard keen on anything new. He had earned his PhD for his work on leptospirosis in dogs, and had actually become infected himself for a short time with this disease. The students nicknamed him "The well-known reservoir host" of the disease. He became very interested in the electrocardiogram (ECG) which was now in use in animals. Of course with the good doctor, everything for a while was ECG. We had an Arab horse with an incipient heart block which was his pet subject. I asked him one day what he would do now that he had this diagnosis.

He retorted, "Is diagnosis not important to you?"

I replied, "Of course but what about prognosis and treatment."

He was mad at me so I thought I had better learn all I could about ECG as it was sure to be in our class exams in medicine. I did not want to be considered a "smart alex" so I went to our physiology lecturer who was an MD and an extremely clever man. He was later given a Nobel Peace Prize for his work on beta blockers for heart disease and a drug for stomach ulcers. He quickly explained to me the reasons for the various parts of the ECG recording, and why they appeared as such. He confessed that there was no explanation for the T wave being above the base line, as it should really be a negative deflection below the line. To remove any doubts concerning my interest in ECG I asked our lecturer about this phenomenon. He was extremely interested and said he would find out the reason. A few days later he told me confidentially that there was no legitimate explanation and we just accepted it. From then onwards he made a habit of asking me in class if I had any questions. There was no doubt I was now out of his bad books. You could never doubt his sincerity or his avid desire to teach us the latest in technology. It reminded me of Oliver Goldsmith's poem, "The Deserted Village", where he describes the village schoolmaster:

A man severe he was . . .
But if in aught
the love he bore to learning lay at fault.

On one occasion he scheduled the post-mortem of a cow for a Wednesday afternoon and we were *all* to attend. Of course, Wednesday afternoon was the only time we were allowed a break from classes. It was a well recognized practice throughout every faculty of the university. In defiance about eight of us crammed into old cars or motorcycles and left for Balloch — a nice little town on Loch Lomond about forty-five minutes away. We had a good time there and it made a nice break. We soon discovered our lecturer was furious. He had already set a class exam paper and immediately asked other lecturers to change the questions and provide the most difficult ones

they could make. He also set two questions on the condition
of the cow which had been revealed to the class in post-mortem
examination. We soon discovered the nature of the condition
of this cow from our classmates and when the examination
was given a few days later, we were better prepared than those
who attended the post-mortem. I also had an idea what the
other lecturers would select and came prepared. I was happy
when I read the examination paper. I did very well and topped
the class by ten marks. I gave my lecturer his due, he was very
complimentary to me despite my absence from his special class.
In a way he was a most useful lecturer, as he stimulated you
to study the most up-to-date methods of diagnoses. When I
look back on my studies, I believe his lectures made me think
for myself and consider various diagnoses, which is essential
when you are faced with a dumb sick animal and an owner
who is not always reliable, or may have a preconceived
diagnosis of his own.

We also had an assistant lecturer in medicine who was very
practical in his approach, if less academic. They proved a nice
balance as far as I was concerned.

Our lecturer in reproduction and obstetrics was a real actor.
He could have gone on the stage. He could mimic all the
sounds of sows and had been an old farm-animal practitioner.
He was not too scientific but very practical and sound in his
approach. I recall my first calving case when I was doing a
locum (temporary substitute) in East Anglia. It was fairly straight
forward, and all I had to do was give the cow a little help. I
first made sure that the calf had a clear air passage, and held
it up by its hind legs to get rid of any foetal fluid. I rubbed
it down and laid it beside the mother's head, where she could
lick it. I removed any supernumerary teats which were blind

and would never be functional. I propped the cow up on each side with straw bales, and I gave her a bucket of water with minerals in it to give her replacement therapy. I also placed an antiseptic pessary in her womb to combat any infection. After, I made sure that there was not another calf waiting to be delivered. It can be very embarrassing if you are recalled to remove a second calf. My last advice was to ensure the cow's comfort.

I had not thought much more about the job until I returned to the surgery, where my boss greeted me with obvious delight. He had just had a call from the farmer to say how careful I had been, and he would send me out anytime to his farm. I thought of my old obstetrics lecturer and his insistence on attention to detail. He deserved the credit and not me. I guess I had adopted the same attitude during my service in Burma, when a mine or booby-trap, or both, together had to be examined and neutralized. The only difference there was that an oversight or careless mistake could be fatal.

As my studies progressed and I entered my final year, I was more and more consumed by the vast field of knowledge. When you are so interested your mind is like a sponge. However, with all the diseases of seven different species – horse, cow, sheep, pig, dog, cat and chicken it was an onerous task indeed, and at times one had to be selective in one's choice of studies. Examinations could cover almost any disease or subject, and guessing those likely to be presented in our examinations was not a wise practice. However, I did employ one useful method.

Final professional exams in each subject at the end of the year are generally conducted by a visiting lecturer from another college, together with your own professor or senior lecturer in that subject. I remember in physiology, I asked my lecturer who the external examiner would be. He replied so and so from some other college. I casually said, "He is a liver man", meaning liver function was his main interest in research. I was quickly told, "No, he is a kidney specialist." Our written paper normally had eight questions and half of these were set by the external examiner, so you could bet your boots there would be at least two on the kidney – there were actually three. I made sure I was very well prepared on kidney functions – far above what I had been given in class. There are three parts to each final examination – written, practical and oral. There is a 50% chance of getting the oral from the external examiner, and in this case there was an excellent chance of being grilled on kidney physiology. My hunch paid off and I was grilled on kidney function by the external examiner and he progressed well beyond our required knowledge. He finally stumped me on the type of substances used to assess kidney function. I did not know their names but I said I would use something which penetrates both extracelluar and intracellular fluid, such as urea. The answer was not what he wanted, but nevertheless was a logical response. He was delighted and my own internal examiner was also very pleased. Alas, the next student for oral examination was not well prepared for routine questions in kidney physiology and he failed. That was something I had not planned and I felt bad about it. Still, in veterinary medicine you need all the help you can get; and you are very much dependent on your own devices.

My big day finally arrived in June 1955 and I was to receive my degree in the large Bute Hall of Glasgow University. I was allowed only two tickets for friends to attend the ceremony. I gave one to my girlfriend and one to my old mother. My

Glasgow landlady had a friend in the University Office, and she obtained one for herself. My father had passed away at the start of my studies. I am sure he would have been proud of me – he left school at 11 to go to work. I was very proud to have my old mother see me receive my degree. She had raised six sons and six daughters, and I was the only one able to finish high school and go on to University. I think it made up for the day when I had to come home from University and tell her I was very ill with pulmonary tuberculosis. I had three women with me on that great day – my old mother who had cared for me, my Glasgow landlady who had also been good to me during my studies, and my girlfriend, a nurse, who would later become my wife. It was quite a change from my army service where men were the important players. Now I owed a great debt to these three women in my life, and I was glad to have them present at my graduation.

As soon as I received my degree I was off to work as a locum in an agricultural practice in East Anglia. I expected to make enough money during the summer to be able to take a postgraduate degree at Edinburgh Veterinary School. I worked in another practice in Devonshire for the same purpose. Unfortunately, although I had actually saved some money from my undergraduate FET allowance, I had nowhere near enough to last me a whole year at Edinburgh. I tried different sources for money and finally wrote to the Animal Health Trust which raises money for animal research and welfare. I stated my case very plainly to this organization, and was delighted when they asked me to send them a budget for my studies. They stressed it must be detailed. I complied by detailing all my expenses, even down to the cost of haircuts. They must have been impressed, as I received far more than my budget.

I was soon accepted at Edinburgh for my course in State Medicine. My plans were falling nicely into place. This post-graduate year passed very quickly and was a valuable addition to my training. I remember my oral examination on meat inspection and hygiene. The external examiner showed me a bovine pancreas with chronic tuberculosis lesions. Of course my interest in tuberculosis was intense and my knowledge of it had been augmented far beyond the class requirements. He was impressed. He then showed me a bovine heart with a tapeworm cyst in the heart muscle. I was very lucky as I had recently written a small paper on this subject. Near my home town there was an ex-POW camp now occupied by European voluntary workers, who were really displaced Europeans, due to the ravages of war in Europe and the Ukraine. These refugees worked on local farms. Some of them had tapeworm infestation which I learned from my local doctor. The sewage system of their camp was inadequate and seagulls frequented the sewage lagoons. In addition, detergents were now in vogue in house-holds and masses of froth were common on these lagoons. This froth was frequently wind borne onto neighbouring farms. It was not difficult to explain the increased local incidence of these tapeworm cysts in cattle heart muscle. My examiner was delighted with my interest in this condition and rapidly granted me a high pass mark in meat hygiene. My lecturer thought I had been lucky. If I had passed it on as his idea, I am sure it would not have been luck. There were only four of us taking this course, and like it or not it is competitive and they seldom pass everyone.

One of my classmates was an Irishman who had worked for the Veterinary Colonial Service in Africa. He was like many Irish, very friendly and full of stories. He had actually met an old native in a village in Africa, who had met Dr. Livingstone, the famous Scottish missionary and explorer. This native claimed Livingstone could take out his brains from his head. Actually he described Livingstone washing his hair with loads of lather at the edge of a lake. My colleague quickly retorted that was the cause of one of our very bald lecturer's problems – too much washing of his hair! My friends tales of darkest Africa were very interesting. One of our very important studies was the control of foot-and-mouth disease. This is the most contagious disease known to man. In the UK the restrictions and government forms to be completed are excessive. My friend described an outbreak of the disease in Africa, where the only measure taken was the deliberate spread of the disease by injecting the nostrils of all cattle with a few ccs of blood, taken from a cow in the outbreak with a high temperature. The disease soon ran its course as it would naturally without intervention from man, and was soon all over. Not one official form was used in this outbreak.

Anthrax is another animal disease communicable to man. Affected animals are slaughtered and burned. In Africa my classmate assured me that a boiled anthrax spleen was a delicacy among the natives – who boil everything. We were always a bit suspicious of the fried black blood-pudding which is commonly eaten in Scotland.

This course in Veterinary State Medicine was a very interesting learning experience, and provided a valuable addition to my veterinary training.

During the first postgraduate year there is an annual competition, open to all graduates of that year of the veterinary schools in UK and Ireland. It requires a thesis on a subject designated by the Royal College of Veterinary Surgeons, the governing body of the veterinary profession in the British Isles. For my year it was "The Part Played by the Vaccination of Animals in Preventive Medicine". Since, much of this knowledge was still fresh in my mind, I did not require very much research to be able to put together some interesting facts and observations. I was delighted to receive Second Prize, The Williams Walley Prize, plus £50. Just what I needed. Later my old Glasgow Veterinary School Principal informed me I would probably have received the First Prize for my thesis, except for the poor typing and presentation of my paper. I explained I just did not have the money to get it professionally typed. He would have offered to get it typed at the College, but I felt that would be unethical, as it was supposed to be my own work. He informed me one examiner was opposed to giving me any prize because of this, but it was decided by the committee that the content really deserved a prize, if not First Prize.

Sometimes it does not pay to be too ethical, but my conscience was clear and my paper now resides in the Royal College Library in London, which is the best honour I could have. It was re-typed at my expense.

CHAPTER 5

Postgraduate Work

Before completion of my course at Edinburgh I applied for a post in the government Ministry of Agriculture Veterinary Investigation Service. In this service there was a central laboratory at Weybridge in Surrey (the largest veterinary laboratory in the world at that time), plus a dozen or so small provincial laboratories throughout England and Wales. The interview was in London and I gained a post in this service as an AVIO (Assistant Veterinary Investigation Officer). Due to the war this was my first full-time job and I was now 32 years old. I was, however, paid according to age plus an extra increment for my DVSM degree and I was thrilled – I had never had so much money. In addition, I also received a whole year of laboratory training at Weybridge with instruction from experts in each veterinary field. I could not have been happier. At the end of my one-year course the Director of Weybridge offered me a job as a research officer, which I declined as I really wanted to get out into the field and get my feet wet. Being an AVIO was a much better challenge, with about fifty veterinary practices to be covered throughout five English counties. In addition to providing routine laboratory diagnostic tests, almost any new disease or condition in animals and poultry was encountered.

On completion of my one-year course I got married and then moved to the East Midlands of England to take up my position at a Veterinary Investigation Centre. I could now apply the ample training I had received; and I was, as they say, close to all the action. I believe the five years I spent there were the most interesting years of my professional life and the most challenging and rewarding. One of my younger colleagues, who had been working there for two years and had never done any service in the forces, complained that my salary was higher than his own. I advised him to spend four years in the army then he would get four increments in pay when and if he returned to the job. He was anti-war, anti-atom bomb, and anti anything else which did not benefit him personally and immediately. Needless to say, he was not impressed by my suggestion. I was to discover that this branch of government service was full of such "D-Day Dodgers" as we called them; and they all had years of seniority over me. In this government service, seniority was the major factor for promotion.

The funds available for research on human health greatly overshadow those available for research into animal diseases, despite the fact that there is generally quite a spin-off in knowledge from veterinary to human medicine. During the five years I spent at this laboratory in the East Midlands, new conditions or diseases in livestock were often brought to my attention for diagnosis and advice on treatment. This presented a real challenge to me and work was never dull or uninteresting. The new or unusual diseases I encountered were too numerous to record here, but I will describe a few of the more interesting ones in this book.

In 1959 we had a very warm dry summer in Lincolnshire. I encountered a whole herd of grazing beef cattle which were all displaying various degrees of lameness. Of course, first of all, foot-and-mouth disease had to be quickly excluded as the cause. On examination there were no obvious signs of infectious disease, and my attention turned to their nutrition. These animals, as was usual, were receiving no supplements – only grazing. Their fields were bare and parched although they had ample acreage to graze. Their gait showed crossing of the forelegs, like scissors. I took some blood samples and sent them for mineral analysis, especially phosphorus. I soon confirmed the first case in the UK of a disease, Stiffsecte, seen in South Africa which was due to severe phosphorus deficiency on good grazing. The remedy was simple – we fed them some bone meal supplement. I obtained the services of a Ministry of Agriculture commission man from London and we made a short cine-film of the disease for teaching purposes. My boss accompanied me for this task and he later presented this film as his work for membership at the Research Club of Cambridge. I was not even invited or mentioned in his presentation – so much for ethical behaviour!

It came to my attention that stillbirth and abortion in pigs was fairly common in this area, and by and large the cause was not often diagnosed. I decided I would try to correct this and make a special study of it. Soon veterinary practitioners were only too pleased to supply me with material. I discovered that the possible causes were many e.g., bacterial, viral infection, nutritional disorders, genetic, hormonal, and immunological causes. I had planned to write a thesis on this work, but unfortunately circumstances prevented this.

In the course of this work I uncovered a viral disease, Aujesyky's disease, in pigs in Lincolnshire. It caused encephalitis and was the first confirmed case in the UK. It presented a serious threat to the pig industry in the UK, and I tried my best to convince the regulatory officials in London, to eradicate the disease by slaughter similar to that for foot-and-mouth disease. Alas, my advice was ignored by the powers that be in the higher echelons. However, within a year or two Aujesyky's disease in pigs was increasing and then made a notifiable disease in swine. To date it must have cost millions of pounds in compensation for slaughter of affected herds. In the words of Robert Burns – "The best laid schemes o' mice and men, gang aft a-gley, and leave us nought but grief and pain, for promised joy." In this case the pigs shared the grief, and the tax payers the pain.

In one area close to the laboratory, I discovered a peculiar condition in new-born piglets. They had markedly thickened forelegs right from birth and were unable to walk. At first it seemed to suggest a genetic defect; but as I found it in other fairly widespread areas in unrelated herds, I began to consider other causes. It did not appear to be infectious in origin and had never been seen before over many years of pig-breeding in the area. I concluded that the common factor may be in the diet, which I then examined in detail. The only common factor was the feeding of swill, in which there was a surplus of discarded bread or biscuit meal. This in turn suggested flour as a factor. I discovered that when dough was made for loaves of bread, it was being treated to render it more kneadable and white. The agents used for this were kept secret, but I suspected that agene gas was a possible ingredient. I wanted to set up a small experiment to confirm or refute this as the cause, but my requests were refused and I could not record the disease without this research. I did the next best thing and told the local veterinarians and pig breeders to discourage the feeding of bread and biscuit meal to pregnant swines – so much for controlled research and politics.

My interest in stillbirth and abortion in swine, led me to investigate the same condition in sheep. In the East Midlands sheep farming played a major role in agriculture. The known causes of abortion in sheep were bacterial and viral. There were also others of unknown aetiology. However, on routine examination of aborted lambs, we often drew a blank. I then decided to look for other infectious causes, and toxoplasmosis came to mind. This is a very small protozoan parasite which infests many species, especially rodents, cats, pigs, sheep and humans. To confirm this diagnosis it is necessary to obtain infected brain tissue from aborted lambs, and passage it through mice. There is also a dye test, which can be done on blood. I discovered that in Boston, a town on the east coast in the flat fen land, the local human population had a high dye test positive incidence. A study of a number of outbreaks of abortion in sheep showed that toxoplasmosis could exist along with other known causes of abortion; but in a significant number of flocks it was the only pathogenic organism present, and it appeared to be the cause of abortion on its own in many flocks throughout the East Midlands. I recorded this study in a paper in the *Veterinary Record* in 1962, as I considered it added weight to toxoplasmosis as a definitive cause of abortion in sheep.

I intended to examine sows for toxoplasmosis and try to cause abortion by infecting them during pregnancy. However, I could not find sows with a negative blood test for toxoplasmosis. It may well be that it is a factor in abortions in swine also. I tried to get permission to research the incidence in women in the town of Boston, as I believed it could be a factor in human abortions. My requests were turned down as too sensitive and encroaching into human research – a typical Civil Service response.

Swine fever (hog cholera) is a serious contagious disease of swine. It is rapidly lethal and is a notifiable disease in the UK, i.e., its occurrence and control must be passed to the Ministry of Agriculture. Normally all swine in an infected herd are slaughtered and burned; and the premises thoroughly disinfected, then rested before restocking can be undertaken. In 1962 in Lincolnshire I was called to a farm by the local veterinary practitioner, where small piglets were suffering from pneumonia. This was the farm of a well-known breeder whose pigs were all vaccinated routinely with the approved crystal violet vaccine for swine fever and who showed his sows at various livestock shows around the area.

It became apparent to me on post-mortem of the affected piglets, that they had a viral type pneumonia, but *not* like the common virus pneumonia seen in pigs, which was widespread in England at that time. Microscopic examination of the affected lungs confirmed my suspicions of a viral-type pneumonia, but *not* like the common viral pneumonia of pigs. All the recognized signs and symptoms of typical swine fever were absent. Normally the presence of typical swine fever can be confirmed by a gel-diffusion test on pancreatic tissue from an infected pig. In this case I dispatched some pancreatic tissue and some of the related lymph nodes from the lungs, to the central laboratory at Weybridge.

The Chief Veterinary Officer of the Ministry of Agriculture discovered that I had included the lymph nodes for testing and complained to the Director of laboratory services at Weybridge.

As it turned out these lymph nodes proved positive for swine fever and the pancreas was negative. In my defence the Director of Weybridge Laboratory informed the overall Veterinary Chief of the Ministry of Agriculture that I probably had good reason for my actions and anyway the result was all important. I had thought long and hard about these vaccinated sows, being exposed at various agricultural shows to other swine. I also knew that the vaccine was made by attenuating the virulent virus in the blood from sows given the disease at Weybridge Laboratory. It was my belief that the field virus encountered by the sows may have undergone attenuation in potency, or these sows may have encountered a modified swine fever virus from sows at livestock shows. Of course the crucial test would be if tissues from these piglets could be injected into healthy pigs and produce swine fever.

Here I was fortunate, as I had known some research workers at Weybridge Laboratory during my training and I convinced them to passage this material from these piglets through normal pigs. The first attempt failed, and tissues taken from these test pigs failed a second time to produce swine fever. However, on the third passage the injected pigs developed typical swine fever. There was no doubt my theory had been confirmed. This herd had an atypical form of swine fever which could ultimately become increased in virulence to produce typical swine fever. I wrote this case up and published it in the *Journal of State Veterinary Medicine*. A short time later the Australians also reported a similar atypical form of swine fever. After a while the Ministry of Agriculture embarked on the eradication of swine fever from the UK.

I know from some colleagues that this herd of swine in Lincolnshire was often quoted during meetings on the progress of eradication of the disease. I had of course warned those in charge that there could be the danger that if they ignored this atypical form of the disease, they could eradicate the disease but leave this virus to spread and perhaps regain virulence. I often think that if I had not used my initiative, but followed the rules like a good Civil Servant, the progress or success of complete eradication of the disease may well have been severely delayed. The Chief Veterinary Officer who had criticized my actions received a knighthood. I never even received a word of thanks for my initiative. I was obviously not a good Civil Servant, and probably never would be!

A short while after this incident the powers that be decided to divide the grade of Assistant Veterinary Investigation Officer into Class I and Class II, with a rise in salary level for those at Level II. I heard via a friend that I was going to be promoted to Level II. Somehow, this was passed by someone to the Director of Weybridge and he was angry that I knew. He sent for me to see him at Weybridge and along with his deputy he interviewed me, and wanted to know who had told me in advance about my promotion. Of course I declined to tell him my source. I was being treated like an errant school boy instead of a professional man. To my regret they rescinded my promotion, despite all my hard work and record of achievements. It was quite obvious they did not value the efforts and accomplishments, I had deserved more than some petty disclosure of a promotion. It was clear I would never make a good Civil Servant in their judgement. One's fate often rests in some peculiar hands! I decided to move to another job. Though having really enjoyed the challenge of this work, there was no way I would be humiliated in this manner, and my prospects were now not very bright.

I set about finding another job, and I soon landed a job with a large pharmaceutical company and set up for them a small working laboratory from scratch to handle work on their new antibiotics. All went very well for over a year, and I was asked to prepare a publication on the results. I, of course, included the fact there were already strains of bacteria resistant to these new drugs. I was told to remove this evidence from my paper, I refused, as it would only be a matter of time until someone else recorded this resistance. My boss offered to put his name on my paper with the resistance deleted. The next day I was called to the company head office and fired without any explanation.

Having just bought a new house for my family, and with my small daughter just started at a new school, this was a serious reverse. Sometimes you have to pay dearly for your principles. I could have gone to the Royal College of Veterinary Surgeons to plead my case, but it would not have altered the outcome, and it would have taken too long. I remember well coming home at noon that fateful day, to tell my wife I was out of a job. This meant I had to sell my home and move to another job, if I could find one. I decided to retrace my steps and have a good look at everything that had happened. I still maintained I had done the honourable thing. After all I had taken an oath when I qualified at Glasgow University, to uphold the honour of the veterinary profession. Wasting no time at home, I prepared my house for sale and managed to obtain temporary work tuberculin testing cattle for the Ministry of Agriculture. This meant being away from home, but it gave me a chance to apply for other jobs. At this stage I was rather bitter about my treatment in England, and tried to join the Veterinary Investigation Service in Scotland. Unfortunately, I discovered that it, also, was controlled from London.

I applied for jobs in Australia, New Zealand and Canada, knowing full well that it would be a slow government process. After about three months I had simultaneous acceptance from all three countries. The Australian job was my first choice, but unfortunately the offer arrived, along with plane tickets for my family, on the very day I left to sail to Canada. I found out later from an Aussie attending one of our Canadian courses on exotic diseases that there was an administrative mix-up in Perth, Australia, which caused this delay. Apparently the administrator was told by his Chief Veterinarian to offer me the job *at once*, but he went on holiday and left it in his in-tray. I believe he was fired by his boss. In any case I was off to Ottawa in Canada with only a few suitcases. Our furniture would follow by freighter.

My mother was 81 years old, and as I said farewell to her, I knew it would probably be for ever. She was in the permanent care of my sister and in excellent hands. I left my native land with a heavy heart. After giving up so much of my young life in the army in the Far East, for my country, surviving tuberculosis, and doing very well at university, then working hard for the government and making a good contribution to veterinary medicine, I was unable to get a viable post in Scotland, due to dominance by the English establishment. It was now time to head for a land of opportunity.

CHAPTER 6

The Joys of Veterinary Practice

After obtaining my veterinary degree in June 1955, I was engaged in temporary assignments or locums in both small animal practice and farm animal practice. Much of this work is routine but nevertheless some interesting, poignant or amusing incidents are worth recording.

General veterinary practice can be compared to general medical practice; but in effect there are quite considerable differences. You deal with the male and female of all domestic and sometimes exotic animals and birds which all have their own specific diseases and conditions as well as common diseases. You can obtain a history of disease only from the owners, who can sometimes mislead you if they already have a preconceived idea of the cause of the condition.

You deal with all types of owners from dear old ladies to astute farmers or owners of racing animals. Also, you may not always have the help you need or the equipment to do the job. You may be dealing with the life of a beloved pet or the livelihood of a poor farmer. The calls for assistance may come at any time of the day or night, on any day of the year. Your patient can be in a dark unlit shed or in the middle of a field on a cold winter night. You can't call an ambulance and ship the animal off to hospital or refer it to a specialist. You are on your own.

You are challenged to obtain a useful history of the animal, then by clinical examination reach a diagnosis and institute some appropriate treatment and advice for the owner. In a sense you often have to treat the owner as well as the animal. If you are called in the middle of the night and need to perform a Caesarean section to save the life of a valuable cow and its calf, you can expect to receive much less for your efforts than a dentist doing a simple crowning of a tooth.

The non monetary rewards are quite different. You may save the animal's life and coincidentally keep the farmer in business, or make a pet owner very happy and grateful. Of course, you cannot win them all and sometimes the animal has been left beyond help. However, win or lose, your efforts often command gratitude and respect from the owners which can be very satisfying.

I remember seeing an article on the public perception of different professionals and their grading. It was no surprise to me to see practising veterinarians at the top of the list even above doctors and clergymen. The lawyers who often deal with conflict, crime and grief came last, which was not surprising.

Of all the domestic animals I consider the cat to be the most interesting. They are highly intelligent, very aloof and can be very determined and resourceful. The alley cat will defend its kittens to the death if necessary and will sacrifice everything for their survival. They can be amusing also.

I recall one very large black tom-cat being brought for boarding for three weeks during its owner's vacation. This old lady gave me detailed instructions to feed her cat pancakes, but only pancakes purchased from a local Co-operative Society bakery. I agreed. Normally we fed our cats on codfish and brown bread stew. This cat flatly refused to eat our highly nutritious diet. As the days past it slowly and visibly melted in condition. About one week or so before the owner's return

I bought some pancakes from the bakery next door. Alas, the cat declined these freshly baked treats. In desperation I went to the Co-operative store and bought a few pancakes. To my astonishment it gulped these down heartily. A second visit to the Co-op assured the restoration of the cat's condition, much to the owner's delight. To this day I believe this animal would have starved rather than eat anything else. It was a very determined animal.

On another occasion, going to see an old tom-cat belonging to an old lady who lived alone, I found the poor creature was lying in the woman's bed and she was sleeping on the floor, so as not to disturb it. Unfortunately, the cat's temperature was subnormal and he was obviously dying. He had been out on the tiles for a few cold wet nights and had severe pneumonia. I explained this to the old lady but she insisted I treat him. I gave it a shot of penicillin just to please her, but it died within a few hours.

I went back next day and offered to have him buried for her for which she was grateful, but very distraught. I had brought a cute little kitten in my car and after comforting her as best I could I brought in the kitten. I told her I had something which she might like and produced the kitten which looked up at her and gave a pathetic little meow. The result was instant joy as the old lady took and caressed the kitten. She wanted to pay my bill but I declined. No money could have ever equalled the joy she received. I knew of course that the old lady would relate all this to her friends and the veterinarian would gain far more in the end.

As a student I once saw practice in a small village with the local practitioner. One day I was asked to collect a cat, to be 'fixed' as we say. I was cautioned by my boss that this was an old maiden lady and I should inquire if the cat was indeed a male. When I inquired the old lady blushed and responded that she did not know if it was a male but she thought it was supposed to be a female. I did a quick check and sure enough it was a male. She immediately asked if it would cost double for both operations. Unperturbed and with a straight face, I assured her only one operation was required and it would cost only five shillings for a male. Sometimes a veterinarian has to be very diplomatic.

In Scotland, anthrax is not unknown among cattle in certain areas. It is of course a notifiable disease and can be fatal for humans in contact with affected animals. I had encountered a steer on a small farm which resembled a case of anthrax. The carcass was conveyed to the local knacker yard for burning. I had made blood smears and sent them to the Minister of Agriculture Veterinary Office for confirmation. I cautioned the old knacker yard owner to be very careful and wash himself thoroughly after handling the animal and to disinfect his truck etc. I was particularly concerned as this old man had a habit of cutting the hides at the tail head and pulling off the skin with his teeth. This was an act of bravado he used to show off to farmers. With this in mind I gave him extra warning and instructions on hygiene. I also instructed him to go to his doctor and receive treatment. About four hours later I thought I had better check this old lad to make sure he was complying with my instruction. When I called his wife she told me he was still in the hot bath and frightened to come out. I had overdone the instructions and had to go and get him and take him out of the bath and down to the doctor's surgery. His doctor commented that he very much doubted that he could have had such influence on his patient.

In Scotland many coal miners keep racing greyhounds to which they are very devoted. They are like a Saint of God sent to make money for them. I remember going to a miner's home to see a sick greyhound. Putting my bag on an armchair I was quickly told, that was the dog's chair. It was the best chair in the house. I also noticed the bath had been adapted with a little ramp for the dog. The bath was full of soft straw where the dog slept. The owner thought this was quite normal.

On another occasion I was called to a greyhound which had been hit by a speeding car. The poor dog had a great V-shaped flap of skin hanging from its side. I tranquillized the poor animal and cleaned up the large wound, then sutured the large flap of skin back into position using forty-three stitches on the job. The owner was mostly interested in his dog being able to race well again and I assured him it had a good chance of recovery. He then suggested it would need a new name for the track. I thought for a moment and looked at the long line of sutures and suggested V43. He immediately agreed it would be a good name for a new dog. I heard that it actually won a few races under this new name. I could not have asked for a better result for my work.

Most animals will make a nest in some secret or secure place, in which to have their young. Dogs do this prior to whelping. I remember being called to a collie bitch on a farm which had prepared a nest with an old piece of blanket, under the kitchen sink. There was one problem – she had never been mated.

I examined her and she had milk in her breasts and was nursing an old fashioned scrubbing brush and a kipper (a dry smoked herring which represented her pups). She had a pseudo-pregnancy which can occur in dogs. They have everything but the pups. It was all in her head, as we say. To cure it you give a large dose of Epson Salts to bring her back to normal and remove the milk. This was a difficult diagnosis to explain to a farmer. Generally, they want to know if women can be similarly affected.

Sometimes you can encounter unusual requests. I remember going to a small remote farm away up in the Scottish highlands. In order of priority I examined a ram with a very severe foot infection. After carefully paring away the dead horn from the foot I dressed it and gave systemic antibiotic by injection. Next I had to look at the shepherd's dog which had bruised its hind leg on a fence.

Lastly I was asked to have a look at the wife who had hurt her knee. Of course I explained she must see a doctor. To no avail. The shepherd insisted that veterinarians were perhaps more knowledgeable than doctors and I should look at her knee. I reluctantly agreed and soon discovered she had been kneeling down to paint the skirting of her kitchen and had knelt on something sharp like a nail. She had an old fashioned house-maid's knee with all the oedema associated with it. The remedy was simple advice not to kneel on it for a long while. I gave her a tube of very nice soft udder cream for chapped teats in cattle to rub on the sore area. It was safe and could cause no harm at all. During the next few weeks I had requests for more of this cream. I was curious to learn why all this cream was required. I discovered it was being used for all sorts of things, even hair-cream by her sons. I tried it on my own hair − it was as good as any hair-cream.

In agricultural practice you cannot carry everything you required in your car. Invariably, you are out of something when you need it, or you have forgotten to replace it after you used it last. I remember going to an emergency calving case. The cow had been trying to deliver her calf for quite some time, much longer than the owners would admit. The birth canal was all dried up and a very large bull calf was still inside. It was quite obvious that all the natural lubrication was lost and had to be replaced. Having nothing suitable with me, I asked the farmer's wife if she used Lux soap powder for her washing and with luck she did. Lux was a fine soft flaky substance which was very slippery when wet and dissolved slowly. I quickly borrowed a whole box of it, placed handfuls all around the calf as far as I could manage. After a few minutes we applied some pull to the hind legs as it was a breech presentation and to my relief we extracted a live but rather dazed and shocked bull calf. The farmer was delighted but I still had to advise him not to wait so long next time before calling for assistance or he may not be so lucky.

On another occasion I was faced with a problem where the uterus or womb of a cow had prolapsed after calving. It was very swollen and oedematous (water logged) and could not be pushed back inside the cow. Again I was out of the necessary drugs to combat oedema and time was short. Then I had a good idea. Borrowing a large bag of fine granulated sugar from the farmer's wife, I spread it over the prolapsed womb and the hydroscopic action of the sugar removed much of the fluid from the womb, sufficient for me to be able to return it to its proper position, then I could relax the muscles and keep it in place. The farmer thought I was something of a genius but in reality it was a gamble which came off. One very good lecturer at college told us we must always be prepared to improvise in emergencies. He had taught me well.

Of all domestic animals the pig is the most difficult to handle, especially if it is a large boar or a sow. They possess tremendous power and can deliver a severe bite or slash with their tusks. To obtain blood or urine samples from them for examinations demands special techniques. Today we have wire snares with strong handles which enable you to control the animal when this is applied to their mouth and upper jaw. Once snouted you can secure them to a rail or post. Blood is best taken from an ear vein. Generally, I would place an elastic band over the root of the ear, then slap the ear a few times or apply some hot water to being up the vein, sufficient to pass a large needle into it and collect the blood sample. This was generally accompanied by loud squeals and snarls from the donor. For urine samples I used an old trick. I allowed the sow out into a yard then splashed its rear end with water. Generally they obliged and a sample was collected in a jar within a few seconds.

When castrating piglets it is essential to remove the sow to a safe secure place before proceeding, as the piglet's squeals will bring an irate mother upon you with murderous intentions.

Poisoning cases are often very challenging. The poison can be easily detected by most laboratories but, of course, the source of the poison must be established or the toxicity will continue. It can require some detective work. Generally, the epidemiology -circumstances surrounding the outbreak, must be studied. I recall a case of lead poisoning in young cattle which suddenly appeared in a field which had been grazed for many years. Obviously the contamination had recently occurred. I examined the whole field without success until I noticed the animals were housed in a very old railway carriage at one corner of the field. There had just been a windstorm and some of the roofing felt had been blown off on to the field. Sure enough, being a very old roofing felt, maybe 50 or more years old, it was laced with lead. Generally, you look for old car batteries or discarded red lead paint cans but in this case, drew a blank. To prevent further losses the roofing felt was replaced by plastic sheeting and any scraps of felt were gathered up and removed from the pasture.

In Derbyshire in England lead was mined and the tailings or rakes are still around but covered by grass. During a severe drought the pastures were so denuded that grazing lambs turned their attention to the old lead rakes and lead poisoning developed. Again the weather had a crucial role in the toxicity.

Arsenic poisoning, also, is occasionally seen in farm animals and the source is not always easy to find. Once, suspecting it in sows at pasture on a farm, I forwarded samples for testing to the central veterinary laboratory in England. My request was questioned with some derision. However, when the samples were found positive the attitude changed. It took me a little time to find the source. The farmer had dipped some sheep with a rather old-fashioned sheep-dip he had kept for many years. He emptied the dip when finished into a nearby ditch. It was rather warm weather and the grazing sows had drunk from the same ditch. The case was solved when the ditch water was found to be laced with arsenic. The laboratory chief inquired how I managed to find the source. I just said, "with difficulty."

One another occasion, right inside a government laboratory, I examined a calf which had been housed in a very old wooden building which had been a dwelling. The calves, of course, in boredom chewed at anything available which included very old layers of wallpaper, some of which were green and full of arsenic which at one time was used to produce this colour. I was always amazed at the attitude of the analytical chemists –

always sceptical of your request, and only really interested in the chemistry. Of course the source of the poison was always the main concern for the stock owner. They invariably showed complete surprise if your hunch proved correct.

On occasion you are asked to treat exotic pets and cage birds. I remember being presented with a very sick budgerigar. The old lady who owned it was very distressed as her pet had become very lethargic and its plumage was shedding. There was very little to see so I questioned her carefully. The bird was not eating and I was sure it would soon die. I inquired of any change in its food or environment but drew a blank. I asked if it had previously been very lively and was assured it used to perform all sorts of tricks after it had a gin nip. There was the clue. When the old lady had a drink in the evening she gave her pet a little drop of gin in its drinking water. I explained that just like people, after a drink her pet perked up and became amusing. Unfortunately, alcohol poisons birds and soon it would be pretty sick. She returned in a few days with her dead bird and I did a post-mortem for her. Sure enough it had a hard cirrhotic liver. I don't really know if this event had any effect on her drinking habits but I did assure her that gin should always be taken in small amounts and not on an empty stomach as humans do get the same liver damage from alcohol.

Poultry play a large part in farming. The diseases of poultry and their pathology are a science on their own. Fortunately, you can always sacrifice a few affected birds and do a post-mortem examination, which generally gives direct evidence of a specific avian disease.

Poultry have two very serious diseases which must be reported to the Ministry of Agriculture, fowl plague and New-castle disease which are collectively known as fowl pest. Plague is rare but Newcastle disease is fairly common and sporadic in Europe. Generally, slaughter of all poultry on the farm is mandatory, then thorough disinfection of the premises follows.

I recall one Christmas Day in Suffolk, England, going to a big poultry farm to supervise the slaughter of an entire flock. I had to value the stock for compensation from the government so at least I had a little leeway to provide some consolation to the poor farmer. It was the worst Christmas Day I ever experienced, although the owner treated me to a nice Christmas dinner which is just as well as everywhere was closed for miles around. Not all veterinary work is pleasant or rewarding.

Turkey farming is common in some parts of England. I remember being called to a large turkey farm where the young growing turkeys were infected by a parasite which resides in the trachea. There is an effective drug for this disease but it has to be given in an inhaled form to be really effective. How do you administer such a cure to hundreds of small turkeys.

Fortunately the farmer had a large cardboard box about six feet long and four feet high and wide. We cut a small hole in each end and an inspection hole in the top of the box. We tried a few birds as a dummy run for safety and it worked well. We treated about thirty birds at a time by blowing an electric hair dryer in one end which distributed a fine mist of drug throughout the box. It worked very well and saved almost all of the birds.

I kept remembering my old college lecturer who inspired us to use our initiative. He would have been pleased with my efforts. The farmer of course was extremely grateful for saving his livelihood. In a sense it was like active service during the war. You remember the good times and try to forget the bad times.

CHAPTER 7

The New World

Our voyage in a large liner the *Arkadia* (a renamed Greek ship), was not luxurious, but certainly a big improvement on a troopship. Within ten days we were sailing up the St. Lawrence River to Montreal. The Quebec shore was interesting in that the fields ran in long fenced strips down to the shore. A crew member explained to me that the land was divided up to give access to the river but as French-Canadians multiplied their sons received a share of the land, hence the narrow strips running down to the water. You could even tell which farmers had been the most prolific.

There was a variety of nationalities on board as immigrants – Poles, Hungarians, Germans, a few French and hardly any British. The French-Canadian Immigration Officer came on board at Quebec City and worked all night screening immigrants before we docked at Montreal. He asked to see my small daughter who was only 5 years old and fast asleep. He wrote her name "Mairi" with the correct spelling without my assistance, much to my surprise. He explained that after the battle of the Plains of Abraham, many soldiers of the Highland Brigade had remained in Canada and married French-Canadian girls. To date there were quite a number of Quebecers with Highland names. It was my first experience of Quebecers, and I was impressed. Even my remnants of high school French were understood and well received. I was going to work and live in Hull, just across the Ottawa River, which forms the boundary between Ontario and Quebec. I was now less apprehensive than when I left Scotland.

Our first Canadian home was an apartment in Hull near the English school. My little daughter played with all the French-Canadian children, and despite the language barrier seemed to be very happy. She would invite all her little friends into the building, much to the concern of the manageress. A French-Canadian colleague gave me a lift to and from work every day until I got my own car. I don't think I had ever been made so welcome.

However, my English speaking boss was much less amicable and at times downright hostile. He made it plain to me that I was an immigrant, and he would have preferred a Canadian-born colleague. He was not very helpful in matters related to work. My main function was to do microscopic examination of various animal tissues sent from all over Canada for histopathological diagnosis. Most of these came from meat inspectors, coast to coast. I enjoyed the work and soon became quite adept at it. After all, your best teacher is often yourself!

One day my boss told me, I was just one of a bunch of bastards from "over there". I replied it was a wise man who knew his own father! On another occasion he told me he was *not* an immigrant. I replied that really in Canada you are all immigrants; at which he responded he was definitely not an immigrant. I then said, "OK, what tribe are you – Mohawk?" His sort were fortunately few and far between, and he was not a happy man. I did my best to do a good job and I ignored his barbs.

The Director knew the situation and advised me to ignore his behaviour. Almost all my colleagues at the laboratory were very amiable and co-operative. One department chief requested the Director to have me transferred to his department. Unfortunately, they had no replacement for me and I was stuck. However, work was interesting and we had a few lighter moments from time to time.

A city zoo had a problem with tuberculosis in some animals, and I had to do post-mortem examinations on several species – African buffalo, leopard, tree kangaroo and a baboon. Some of the animals were transported live to Hull. Removing them from the truck and anaesthetizing them proved a challenge. The buffalo could not be killed by the humane-killer pistol, as their skulls were too thick; so I gave them an intravenous lethal dose via the ear vein or jugular. I had great difficulty finding someone to assist me. My brave boss was conveniently absent. The baboon, a large male, arrived in a big steel cage. I decided to keep it outside the PM room until I could anaesthetize it. I used taped garbage bags to cover the cage, then I ran a tube from a carbon dioxide cylinder into the cage. The animal was soon anaesthetized completely and I gave it a lethal injection of barbiturate. Before I put it to sleep my technician and I had been joking in the PM room. When the baboon outside the door barked we said, "Quiet Julius" (the lab director was called Julius). Unknown to us Julius was standing outside looking at the baboon. Fortunately, Julius, although a fairly serious man, had a good sense of humour.

We had quite an interesting group of professionals at the laboratory – and although there was always a little animosity between a few members, by and large they were a happy group. We all ate lunch in a nice big lunchroom with nice sofas, etc. We had no cafeteria so we packed a lunch. We had all types and nationalities. One Hungarian was a very excitable type. He generally lay down on a large sofa for a little nap after he had been at the trough. One day, when he was asleep we moved all the potted plants around the sofa and doused the lights. We played soft music on a radio and everyone kept quiet. He had a habit of saying whenever anyone gave him a specimen for examination, "Fas iz dis?" Hence he became known as Dr. Fasizdis. When he was sound asleep I crawled under the soft and said softly "Denis you're dead". Soon he awoke and exclaimed, "Fas iz dis". We had felt sure that would be his first response.

I enjoyed working at this laboratory. My relations with all the staff were very cordial, with one exception – unfortunately he was my boss.

Every year our department laid on a veterinary course on exotic diseases on an isolated island in the St. Lawrence estuary. It had been an old quarantine station, Grosse Isle, on which many diseased immigrants from sailing ships were landed and quarantined for treatment. Regrettably, most of these poor souls perished there from cholera, small pox, typhoid and other plagues. They had left famine-ravaged Scotland and Ireland only to find a grave on Grosse Isle. We used some of the original buildings for our course. The students came from all over – UK, USA, Norway, Mexico, Australia, New Zealand, as well as some Canadian government veterinarians.

It was a unique course and had worldwide recognition. I was rather honoured to lecture there and assist with the pathological examination of the test animals. It was also a great experience in human relations with all diverse nationalities participating as students. Somehow, they all seemed to revert to their student days, which meant playing jokes on anyone susceptible. There was never a dull moment. Our director came to visit near the end of the course. We were housed in

the old first-class passenger accommodation. Small single bedrooms with wash-hand basin, and a bed. He woke up in the
night to find a live sheep under his bed – I think the Australians
were responsible. At the end of the course each student had
to describe the disease in the animal cubicle assigned to him
– to give his diagnosis and his rationale. I was supposed to act
as the farmer and ask awkward questions, the way some farmers
often do. No one took offence. It was all good training. On
the last night we had a big farewell dinner, with the usual
speeches which soon degenerated to telling funny stories. It
seemed these are international. I came in for some teasing
about my Scottish accent but I assured them, an accent was a
relative thing, and their accents sounded just as peculiar to me;
and anyway I had the language and they had the accent!

When I was asked for a Scottish story, I told them about
the old Scottish farmer in Quebec, who was not too friendly
with his French-Canadian neighbour. One day while ploughing
his fields he struck a large rock and turned it over to free a
small fairy. The fairy was so pleased to be free, he granted the
old farmer three wishes. However, he warned him that he
knew of his dispute with his French-Canadian neighbour, and
anything he was granted his neighbour would receive double
the amount. The old farmer reluctantly agreed and being
Scottish asked for $100,000. His neighbour would receive
$200,000 as agreed. He was very lonely and for his next wish
he asked for a nice young blonde; and as stipulated his
neighbour would receive two blondes. The old farmer then
considered his last request very carefully like a true canny Scot.
He then enquired of the fairy: "Would it be very painful to
have one testicle removed?" If nothing else they would
remember this story.

At the end of the dinner we toasted the health of the Queen. Then the Norwegian proposed a toast to King Haakon of Norway, and the Mexican proposed a toast to their El Presidente. Not to be outdone the two Americans, who spoke Alabamese, proposed a toast to Senator George Wallace. It was a most memorable dinner and I made many friends from around the world, some of whom I would meet again in Australia and New Zealand.

Later, when I was near to retirement in Canada, I was offered a job in New Zealand for three years, by the Kiwi who had remembered me on the course at Grosse Isle.

In Canada, professional civil servants generally belong to the Professional Institute of the Public Service, which in effect is a trade union. I was elected president of the Veterinarians Group of about 500 members across Canada. At that time collective bargaining was introduced by Prime Minister Trudeau, and our Veterinarians' Group were selected to be first to bargain by our union; mainly because we had done our homework over several months. This proved to be a real experience, and after about three months of talks with the Treasury Board of Canada we had not even agreed on the purpose of the agreement. It was an exercise in futility and the Treasury Board obviously meant to tire us out and frustrate us into a poor monetary increase, which would set a precedent for other groups.

I relayed our troubles to several veterinarians who were inspectors at large meat packing plants and cross border inspection points, and suggested we may soon need to work strictly to rule. This meant the inspection line would be reduced to a crawl. Of course the plant owners soon called the top officials in Ottawa, expressing their concerns over our slow pace of negotiations. Miraculously we were summoned to a new meeting with new Treasury Board negotiators and the wheels began to turn. We soon settled almost every clause of a good collective agreement, and we received about eight per cent increase the first year and seven and a half per cent for the next year, plus other allowances for overtime, etc. I had served my veterinary colleagues well, but my chances of advancement were now about nil.

I was, however, approached by CIDA (Canadian International Development Agency) to take a one-year post in Barbados, where I was to set up and develop a working veterinary laboratory as part of the Comfith Project. This project would establish a meat industry in Barbados, by feeding animals on sugar cane. Canadian engineers had designed a machine to crush sugar cane through rollers and deliver a fine fodder, which with molasses could be fed to animals in feed-lots and produce good weight gains. The island had depended upon sugar production for export, but because of the large cane fields developed in Queensland, Australia, where mechanical harvesting was easy, Barbados could no longer compete very well in this market. Tourism to Barbados had taken over from sugar production, but American tourists like to eat steak which in turn had to be imported at great cost. The Comfith Project was to assist the island to produce good quality cheap meat for tourist consumption. Before I left Barbados this had been achieved by this project. My task was to care for the animals. This did not take up too much of my time and I trained a number of locals to do laboratory work e.g., bacteriological cultures, worm counts, PM examinations, blood sampling and even histological sections.

It was not too difficult as some of these boys had the

equivalent to Cambridge A-levels. They were of course different from the students I had known, but they had a good sense of humour on which I often relied. I was very satisfied with their efforts, and I never hesitated to remind them that one day I would be gone and they would need to run this laboratory on their own. I could not have asked for a better crew. I was also asked to help train a number of local health inspectors, especially in meat inspection. I remember describing the black pigment in bacon from black pigs. This was only melanin pigment and quite harmless. I hesitated to make a joke about it as housewives don't really like this type of bacon. I said, "Gentlemen this is one case where Black is not beautiful!" They all laughed heartily and I knew from then onwards I was well accepted. It was a nice feeling to know you could joke with these strangers.

When my mission was completed within one year I had a real sense of achievement and satisfaction, although it had interrupted my daughter's education. However, she did see how the other half of the world lived, and it was a useful experience. The Barbados government Minister of Agriculture gave me a nice send off and a very nice accolade. Later in Canada I was told this Comfith Project in Barbados was one of their best success stories in their overseas aid programme.

Back in Ottawa I was soon transferred to another post. I was appointed veterinarian to the large Central Experimental Farm of the Department of Agriculture in Ottawa. This complex right in the middle of Ottawa City housed thousands of livestock – cattle, sheep, pigs and poultry, and employed numerous animal research scientists, e.g., animal nutritionists and physiologists. Unfortunately, they had no full-time veterinarian.

I soon established a post-mortem service and also histopathological and bacteriological services. The animal attendants were very good, but had been left very often to their own devices to treat animals. Generally, they overdosed to ensure a cure, which is sometimes counter productive. Fortunately, the Research Director gave me full authority over all animal treatment, which meant most of the animal scientists had to take my advice on treatment of their project animals. This had often to be done tactfully, as animal scientists with PhDs sometimes have never treated animals like a farmer. The stockmen were always on my ride, which meant my treatments were respected, and the Director would not stand for any interference in my work. It was an interesting experience but a seven day per week job with also occasional night work – thrown in.

After about a year I applied for a post in the Bureau of Veterinary Drugs in the Department of Health and Welfare.

I won this competition, and moved back into office work. This work involved the review of experimental trials on new veterinary drugs, submitted by pharmaceutical companies. I was well suited for this type of work, because of my experience in pathology, bacteriology, parasitology and clinical medicine. Most of the studies were done on laboratory animals to ascertain the safety of any drug residues for human consumption in food. Carcinogenicity, teratogenicity and toxicity had to be assessed in comprehensive laboratory animal experiments by the Safety Division of the Bureau of Veterinary Drugs.

Finally, a safety factor for humans for each new drug had to be calculated from the experimental data on toxicity of drug specimens in meat and milk. This task was quite onerous and challenging, and could be very complex. I always thought the general public had little idea of how much work and care went into approving a new veterinary drug. In any case, since I was not a vegetarian, I had a vested interest in this work. I even had to deal with the treatment of honey bees to ensure their honey was safe from drug residues. With the advent of Free Trade between Canada and the USA an agreement on the standards for safety of each animal drug, had to be negotiated. In addition, our methods of assessment of drug toxicity had to be equalized. This process was quite a revelation, but our discussions and negotiations with our American counterparts, could not have been better. Needless to say, it was scientists doing the negotiating and not politicians, and therein lay the difference.

Our American hosts in Washington were always exceptionally cordial and co-operative. We were treated like royalty on many occasions. When we had international meetings on veterinary drugs in Washington, we had excellent co-operation with our American counterparts. I recall being invited to a reception in the State Department in Washington after one meeting.

The pharmaceutical companies who produced the drugs, also had very well qualified scientists. However, governmental officials always had the final say on any regulatory measures on drugs. It was very important not to abuse this power, and always to be fair in assessment, while protecting the public from toxic drug residues in food.

One of the last tasks I performed for Canada, was to represent Canada on a select committee on veterinary drugs at the United Nations (WHO and FAO) in Geneva. Almost all developed nations were represented on this committee, which deliberated for about two weeks on a number of new veterinary drugs.

These representatives were all top scientists in their own country, but discussions were generally very cordial and constructive. The pattern of discussion was almost always the same – the Germans would first give their opinion on a drug, closely followed by the French opinion, then the British would add their comments and then the Australians would deliver their views. The Americans generally said very little, although their system of evaluation of new drugs was probably superior to all others. Canada, of course, was closely in step with the USA, although we had made some changes to this position and had agreed on these beforehand, during periodic consultations.

It was a very interesting experience and very productive. My only reservation was that some members did not really have practical experience of treating animals on a farm, with all that could entail in practical terms. Still, on reflection we all did very well. I often wonder why politicians could not achieve the same consensus at their meetings. I could not help concluding that our system of veterinary drug assessment in Canada compared very favourably with all others.

CHAPTER 8

Down Under

It was now 1988 and I was into my sixty-fourth year, with an eye on retirement. I had not really intended to retire at this time as I was still very active and had a few good years of work left in me. However, one day I scrutinized my pay stub and soon calculated with all my deductions and taxes, that I was in effect working for only half pay. I then estimated my retirement income after taxes and discovered that my present remuneration for working was only very slightly above my retirement income. The only benefit for working was about a two per cent annual increase in my ultimate pension. I decided to retire and leave myself the opportunity to work elsewhere.

I had visited Australia and New Zealand on holiday a few years earlier, and my wife and I enjoyed both countries. I had also met Australian soldiers during the war and despite their brash approach to life, I was quite at ease with them. We decided to apply as a family to emigrate to Australia. We soon realized just how complex this process would become. We had to be reborn! My medical history, due to the war, caused great demands for special medical tests. They wanted to see the inside of my lungs as well as the outside. Fortunately, the specialist physician was very supportive and gave me a clean bill of health. I then had to agree to an annual medical examination in Australia, *if* I was accepted for immigration. No problem.

We sold our small farm and packed our furniture, etc. in a large container. I had a farewell dinner with my workmates on my last day at work, and next morning left for Adelaide in South Australia by air. In Adelaide it was off season for holiday-makers, and we soon found good rental accommodation right across the road from a beautiful beach. My daughter found a job with the South Australian government almost immediately, and we were instant Aussies. I soon discovered that thousands of Asian immigrants were arriving regularly in Adelaide. They obviously did not have to meet all the requirements set for my family. I never did understand the rationale for their easy acceptance, especially when it was quite common to see large signs displaying "Stop the Asian Invasion". There were many nationalities present. The English were commonly referred to as "Whingeing Poms". The word "whingeing" denotes someone always complaining or moaning; and the word "Pom" is a derogatory term for someone from England with a fresh complexion, like a pomegranate skin. The Irish emigrants were "Mick's" and expected to be unruly like the "Wild Colonial Boy", Jack Dougan the outlaw made famous in song.

I decided to look for fellow countrymen and discovered three pages of MacKays or Mackies in the Adelaide telephone book. Now to my added surprise there were fifteen pages of them in the Sydney telephone directory. Up in north Queensland there is a lovely little town on the coast named MacKay and pronounced in the correct manner. I discovered one of the original convicts shipped to Australia to a penal colony, was one Stuart MacKay. Apparently, he was sentenced to deportation for a minor offence and shipped off to Australia, where he was eventually released and told in polite terms to, "Go forth and multiply". Old Stuart did not do too badly when you read the telephone directory and the map of Australia. In reality these seven hundred plus convicts were ideal immigrants. They were strong, fit and healthy. Many were skilled and also adventurous and resourceful. Australians are not great respecters of authority and I believe many of their natural characteristics are attributed to the original convicts. They have a refreshing candour and are amiable and hard working. I always found the Aussie soldier, a Digger, friendly and reliable. Their officers were also much better than our own.

I soon found a job with the South Australian government, their Ministry of Agriculture, doing work similar to that which I had done for the Federal Government of Canada. They really needed my services and there was at least a whole year backlog of work. Very slowly and carefully I introduced the systems and methods of doing evaluation I had used in Canada without encountering any opposition or complaints and things soon began to tick over nicely. I had several female clerks to assist me and have never seen women work so well. Their efforts meant I could review and clear many more new drugs than ever before. Australia was still a very male chauvinistic country, and women were still struggling for equality. As far as I was concerned they were often superior to male workers and a pleasure to work alongside.

At one time the women were referred to as "Sheilas", which was a very derogatory term and is no longer in common use. I explained to them one day that "Sheila" was a very nice and respected Gaelic name and that I once had an old dog called Sheila. They were not amused, so I quickly explained how faithful and precious this old dog was to me. As far as I was concerned there was none better.

The Aussies are very forthright by nature and you either like that or you don't. I much preferred their attitude to that of the English, who tended to be reserved and cautious. It was not difficult to see why so many English immigrants never really made it in Australia and returned home as soon as they could afford it. There was no place in Australia for pretension. One Aussie mate (that is Australian for friend) told me about the different cities in Australia. In Melbourne they ask what school you attended?; in Adelaide, what church you attended?; in Sydney, how much money did you have? In Brisbane and Perth they said, "Come and join us"; but in Darwin, away up on the northern shore, "What are you running from?" It was obvious there were regional differences in such a large country.

As part of my work I had to attend a rural agriculture show or fair, where we had a small exhibit. I set up a microscope with some sheep worm parasites, etc., and was soon very busy especially with the farmers' children. I believe the farming communities around small towns were even more friendly than in the cities. Of course I was referred to almost at once as "Scotch". I tried to explain that there was only one thing Scotch, and that came out of a bottle. This was all done in the best of spirit – if you will pardon the pun! I really enjoyed that day and thought my time was well spent. I had also been able to appreciate rural Australia.

My wife got a job with an oil company as a documentation control clerk, which was similar to her work in Canada. My daughter had a secretarial job in Adelaide and everything was going well for my family. We had a very nice new modern bungalow which had been built for the builder himself to his own design. We also had a nice garden which I could develop. I had great neighbours. We were only ten or fifteen minutes from miles of beautiful sandy beaches. There was only one drawback – occasionally sharks came in close to the shore. Generally helicopters kept watch and chased them back out to sea by flying low over them, and also sounding an alarm. Still, every year some swimmer would be attacked and lose a leg or their life. Many Aussies did not seem to be too concerned and swam out some distance from the shore.

The Aussies love to gamble. It is a national pastime in Australia. I remember on a troop ship some Aussies were even gambling on which seagull would perch on the ship's main mast. We picked up some Aussies at Port Said on the Suez Canal, and they gambled all the way to Bombay. In Australia the famous Melbourne Cup horse race is a national holiday, just like Christmas, New Year and Anzac day. The last is similar to our Remembrance Day in Canada, and is a national holiday with a huge military parade. I watched the parade in Sydney one year while on holiday and there were over 20,000 in the march. I once marched in the Adelaide parade, which was much smaller, but still quite an experience. Australia has the RSL (Returned Servicemen's League) which is a very powerful organization. They have much more clout than our Veterans or Legions in Canada or UK. The RSL has still considerable political clout in Australia. This was not surprising as Australians are very patriotic and respectful of their history. You felt really special as an ex-serviceman in Australia. The Aussies all knew about the Burma campaign and the 14th Army even although their troops did not serve in Burma. I was told that during the war, each evening the news from the various theatres of war, was routinely covered, and Burma always got special mention. I regret that in Canada or the UK, Burma was scarcely ever mentioned.

In addition to my work in Adelaide, I was approached to review some new drugs for the Central Commonwealth Government in Canberra. Some of these drugs I had already reviewed for Canada in Ottawa, so it was no great chore to assist them. They were rather sceptical of anything American so I refrained from any comparisons with the FDA in Washington. It was obvious that American and Australian methods of administration clashed. Considering the great part played by America in the Pacific War, it was hard to understand their animosity towards the USA. I suppose it was due to the fact that the USA was a rich developed nation while Australia was a young but proud developing country with obvious potential. In terms of ethnic roots, both countries had attracted many nationalities except, of course, Australia had almost no Afro-American counterpart. Both countries had indigenous native populations – Indians and Aborigines, although the latter, "Abos" as they were called, were more primitive and isolated. They had been in Australia for over 40,000 years, and had been isolated from modern civilization for most of that time. Like the Indians they suffered badly from the effects of alcohol which they did not metabolize like the white race. However, the Aborigines once removed from his nomadic existence can become well educated. Australia constructed a large centre for Aborigines near Ayres Rock in the centre of Australia. However, the native people declined to live there and reverted to their nomadic existence. I suspect you can't change a 40,000-year-old way of life as easily as that. I hope their culture survives.

Life in Australia was very agreeable, but as is often the case, things can be too good to last. Like most developed nations economic downturn and unemployment became increasingly evident. My wife enjoyed working for a large company, but being fairly new in the company she was laid off. My daughter who had only been able to find temporary work through an employment agency was also laid off. With my pension and salary we were still well off, but for my daughter, long range prospects did not look very promising. We had to make a big decision before house prices fell, or the bottom dropped out of the house market. Reluctantly, we decided to move and return to Canada, where most of our working lives had been spent. I could probably have worked for years in my Australian job, but my main concern was for my family.

We decided, as a family, to return to Victoria, BC After sampling the warm climate of Adelaide, with no snow, Victoria seemed the best prospect in Canada. My wife and daughter left almost at once, and I was entrusted with selling our house and moving our effects. I made my own sale sign and to my neighbours' surprise I sold my house myself to a bank manager without any relator's assistance, within two months. I also packed most of our small effects and sent our belongings by container to Victoria via Tacoma. I also held a large garage sale which cleared out everything else. The new owner of my house kindly put me up for a few days, as he wished to move in quickly. They were a typical Aussie family and were very pleasant and friendly. Selling the house and moving to Victoria was not the difficult operation I had expected. It also gave me the opportunity to show the new owner's family all the little things they needed to know about their new home. I think we all benefited. The new owner and his wife drove me to the airport to see me off. My workmates were also there waiting to bid farewell. I believe it was probably the most sad farewell of my life. It reminded me of my farewell to Barbados where my laboratory staff all came to the airport with gifts to see me off.

The Aussies will always have a special place in my heart.

CHAPTER 9

Service with Five Different Governments on Three Different Continents

Having worked for the government service of the UK, the Federal Government of Canada, South Australia State Government, and Commonwealth Government of Australia and the Barbados Government, you conclude that all five are based on the UK Civil Service structure and protocol.

In principle, the basic civil service structure is a pyramid, where you start at the base line and try to climb as far as possible to near the apex. In effect there are many barriers as you ascend and they can be impenetrable unless you are born lucky or influential. In theory you should possess good academic qualifications, diligence, initiative, honesty and dedication. In reality, the very nature of government service attracts subservient workers who seek job security as a first priority. Their work is often routine, boring and initiative is not expected or rewarded. They are governed by staff regulations as their bible. If you are prepared to be "a good steady chap" you can ascend the ladder to senior positions, especially if you happen to be on the spot when someone retires or croaks. You are rarely judged on any enterprise or innovation you introduce or suggest. However, your supervisor may glean some kudos for your efforts, if he can present them as his own, or as part of his supervision over you. You are seldom fired for incompetence. Your promotion prospects can be reduced if your initiative upsets someone at a very high level who is a career Civil Servant.

You may have heard of the "The Peter Principle" where workers are promoted until they reach their level of incompetence. In reality some people are promoted way beyond that level. It definitely helps to be at the right place at the right time and know how to hold a sherry glass. If you are wearing the "old school tie", you may hear, "We simply must have that chappie." If you make few personal decisions and refer matters to your superiors, you are unlikely to make many mistakes, and you will automatically be a good steady chap, but will be very unlikely to make any significant contribution. Then when it comes to promotion, your supervisors are in judgement of you and may perceive you as a threat to themselves. Every year your supervisor is supposed to make out a progress or performance report on his staff. These reports go on your personal file, and in theory are to be used for selection for promotions. Selection boards are usually chaired by the chief of the unit involved and with assistance from his chosen cronies.

All on the surface appears fair, but in effect it is often a Kangaroo Court, and there is no appeal on their decision. Your supervisor can give you a mediocre annual report, carefully couched in ambivalent terms, if he dislikes your ethnic origin or background, or worse still is afraid of your ability. It is little wonder that the Civil Service does not enjoy high respect from the people they are supposed to serve. Private industry could not be competitive with such managers.

The UK Government Service

The Ministry of Agriculture in the UK has three veterinary divisions. The largest division is the Field Staff, whose function is the control of dangerous diseases, such as foot-and-mouth disease, fowl pest and swine fever. They also control the tuberculin testing of cattle for the eradication of bovine tuberculosis. There activities are fairly routine and boring.

The Research Division is mainly concerned with work on dangerous diseases and their diagnosis and prevention, e.g., fowl pest. They also produce tuberculin for TB testing of cattle, and also swine fever vaccine. These functions are carried out at Weybridge Veterinary Laboratory which is probably the largest veterinary laboratory in the world. The third division is the Veterinary Investigation Service, which has a number of regional laboratories throughout the UK. These provide laboratory services for local veterinary practitioners. This includes diagnostic tests for parasites, infections in milk, including TB, Johnes disease and also a post-mortem service on animals and poultry. New and interesting conditions are also referred to these laboratories for field investigation. The latter was of great interest to me and resulted in my employment in the Veterinary Investigation Service. It was by far the most interesting and challenging work available.

Government veterinary services offered regular salary increments, fixed holidays and sick leave, non-contributory pensions and regular hours of work with many benefits, unlike general veterinary practice, where the hours can be long with little leisure time and holidays. It was little wonder that many graduates chose to enter government service. Unfortunately, many of the best graduates tended to avoid government service. I recall visiting a farm, 100 miles from home one Sunday to check out an interesting outbreak of disease in pigs. The local practitioner was very surprised that I came on a Sunday. I guess his perception of our service was justified. I regret that many of the government staff would have waited until Monday to investigate – unless of course it was something serious such as suspect foot-and-mouth disease. In general we were not held in high esteem by our colleagues or by farmers. I very much regret that government service did not invoke any sense of urgency or dedication or initiative; but I was determined not to leave behind my brains and mind, and work for an OBE. The prospect of waiting on dead men's shoes did not appeal to me, so I decided to move on, although I had enjoyed the challenge of new diseases and conditions in animals and poultry.

Canadian Government Service

Canada had a similar structure of veterinary services to that of the UK, except there were only a few provincial laboratories. Research was mainly carried out in the Central Veterinary Laboratory in Hull (now in Ottawa) and was mainly aimed at diseases under Federal control. Research officers were mainly recruited from UK and they often were given department chief positions. I regret their output of research was poor in comparison to Guelph Veterinary School in Ontario which had fewer workers and less resources.

I believe that Canada was short changed in their recruitment from England, and it did little for prestige of UK veterinary

research. The department of Health and Welfare fared somewhat better with the appointment of professionals from the
UK, although these were mainly chemists and had no veterinary
expertise but functioned mainly as administrators. Unfortunately, the Bureau of Veterinary Drugs was controlled by
chemists. It was my experience that chemists can talk only to
chemists. Nevertheless the Canadian Bureau of Veterinary
Drugs managed to provide an excellent service and was highly
regarded by the US FDA. I well remember their chief telling
me that they just marvelled at the way we performed with a
fraction of the staff they employed. In addition Canada ran a
course on exotic diseases in animals and poultry, which was
the envy of every foreign veterinarian who attended from all
over the world.

Barbados Government Service

During my work for the Department of Agriculture in Ottawa
I was asked by the Canadian International Development Agency
(CIDA) to undertake the development of a veterinary laboratory
connected to a research project on animal nutrition in Barbados.
This was a one-year assignment which really required an experienced laboratory veterinarian to train local technicians. My
wife and daughter would have to come with me and it meant
selling our house in Ottawa. I accepted the challenge and it
proved most rewarding. However, it was a different picture –
black Barbadians were in charge of local government and despite
their lack of training and experience, they did very well to
cope with a new nation. They respected professional knowledge
and were always ready to listen. Their big handicap was lack

of funds. I recall a visit by the Minister of Agriculture to my laboratory. He was genuinely interested in my efforts and in my native staff in training. I explained I had received over 100 applications for two laboratory positions, and many of the applicants had a good education – even Cambridge A-levels. However, he could do little to create jobs. He was able to build only a towel factory to help employment. There was a great need for development capital on the island, which depended heavily on tourism. On my last day of work I was given a farewell dinner and the Minister attended and gave me a very sincere accolade for my efforts. This was far more than I ever received from other governments. I believe the year in Barbados did expose my family to another side of life in the slow lane. It was a useful experience for us all.

Australian Government Service

My stint in Australia was quite interesting. The South Australian State Government was very active. In fact, Australians although very isolated were quite progressive and industrious people. I had one big advantage – I was Scotch (as they referred to me). I was told that the Scots were regarded as the best immigrants. The Aussies complained that the English were unwelcome and after two or three weeks in Australia they became shop stewards and trouble makers or "Whingeing Poms". Their Civil Service was chronically understaffed but at least made great efforts to cope with technical work. There were no passengers as in the UK or Canada; and no "bludgers" as they called freeloaders. I believe of all the five governments for which I had worked, the Australian State Government was the best and most productive. The Aussie spirit of "give him a fair go" or "good on-ya-mate" seemed to prevail in the work place. You either like that attitude or you don't. Generally, freeloaders and passengers don't. It was clear to me that Australia would become an increasingly important nation, as their new national anthem says, "Advance, Australia Fair". There was of course some animosity between the State Government and the Commonwealth Government in Canberra. It was in a way similar to that in Ottawa, London and Washington; although the Aussies were much less subservient to their national government. They were a very independent race, which was not a bad thing, when I recall central administrations. I often thought I would have fitted much more easily into the Australian Government Service than the UK or Canadian Government services.

My dealings with the Commonwealth Government in Canberra, consisted mainly of reviewing veterinary drugs for human safety. I used the "up-to-date" American system for review, as they were just getting into the same type of comprehensive review of drugs. I found them very co-operative, and could have co-operated with them continually had I not decided to return to Canada. Their renumeration for my efforts however worked out less per hour than the typist received per hour for typing my reports. This type of problem with professional workers seemed to be fairly common in Australia.

On reflection of working for all five different governments on three continents, I have to conclude that they all suffer from the same lethargic philosophy. There is always someone higher up who can make a decision for you, or you can write a very non-committal report which will probably be filed away or passed to some mindless bureaucrat for action. I regret action was a rare commodity in government services.

Postscript

I had been working since I was 8 years old and I was now 66. It was time to retire – but where? I was a Canadian citizen and Canada had been good to me. I had spent most of my working life in Ottawa. My family chose the small pleasant, peaceful garden city of Victoria on Vancouver Island, with its even, temperate climate. Here I could garden all year round and there was ample opportunity to do charitable work, and for leisure. Here I could write my unremarkable auto-biography. In this journal I have purposely used humour throughout, as an antidote to the harsh times of Burmese jungle warfare, long hospitalization, and six long years of intensive university study, followed by some career disappointments and disruptions – I hope I have succeeded. Overall my achievements and success more than balanced my misfortunes, for which I am truly grateful.